Creativity in Death Education and Counseling

D1738747

Edited by
Charles A. Corr
Southern Illinois University at Edwardsville

Judith M. Stillion
Western Carolina University

and

Mary C. Ribar
Eastern Intermediate School
Montgomery County, MD

Published by the Forum for Death Education and Counseling
2211 Arthur Avenue, Lakewood, Ohio 44107
© 1983

This book was produced by Ag Press, 16th and Yuma Streets, Manhattan, Kansas 66502.

ISBN # 0-9607394-2-4

Published by

Forum
for Death Education
and Counseling
2211 Arthur Avenue, Lakewood, Ohio 44107

TABLE OF CONTENTS

Preface

PREFACE

The theme of *creativity* is a particularly suitable one for the field of death education and counseling, and for the organization that this volume represents — the Forum for Death Education and Counseling. Sustained attention to issues of dying, death, and bereavement on the part of a large, growing, and diverse array of researchers, educators, caregivers, and counselors is a relatively recent phenomenon. Though continuous with a much older history, it is also a dynamic reaction to a waning and displacement of attention that had intervened. Similarly, the founding of the Forum for Death Education and Counseling in 1976 embodied an innovative attempt to create a means of personal contact and interaction for those working in this field. This volume is merely one expression of the work of those laboring in this field and of the ways in which their efforts can be brought together through the Forum. It is a vehicle through which the creativity inherent in Forum and in its members can be permitted to define itself for the reader.

Annual meetings of the Forum, held since 1978, have led to the publication of two previous collections of papers, *New Directions in Death Education and Counseling* published by the Forum in 1981, and *Priorities in Death Education and Counseling* which appeared the following year. The present volume draws upon papers from the Forum's 1982 meeting in San Diego. In fact, annual meetings of the Forum are broader in the scope of their activities than can be represented here or in any print form. Nevertheless, we believe that these papers constitute a fair sampling both of the San Diego meeting and of current work in our field. It has been our privilege to work with their authors to select and arrange chapters for this book, and to bring it into being. As editors, we alone are responsible for decisions regarding the content of this volume, and we can only express our regret that practical limitations did not permit us to include other desirable pieces.

In addition to the contributors whose work appears here and to many other members of Forum, we wish to express our gratitude in particular to the following:

— to Joan N. McNeil, Forum's president, and to the Forum Board of Directors who authorized and funded this project;

— to John S. Stephenson and Shirley A. Phares who served as Co-Chairpersons of the 1982 San Diego meeting;

— to Southern Illinois University at Edwardsville for academic and moral assistance;

— to Professor Alice S. Demi and the School of Nursing of the Medical College of Georgia who provided practical logistical assistance, and to Deborah Williams who did the hard work of bringing the manuscript into its present final form.

Charles A. Corr
Judith M. Stillion
Mary C. Ribar

SECTION ONE

ORIENTATIONS FOR CREATIVITY

SECTION ONE

ORIENTATIONS FOR CREATIVITY

Two individuals who have set high standards for creativity in their own work in the field of dying, death, and bereavement are the keynote contributors to this volume: Gerald G. Jampolsky and Edwin S. Shneidman. There is much that is different in these two men and in their work. Jampolsky is trained in medicine and psychiatry, Shneidman in clinical psychology. Jampolsky has particularly been involved in work with children and their families, Shneidman in suicidology and the broader issues of thanatology. Though both are well known as lecturers and authors, Jampolsky is especially recognized for his informal speaking style, his own book Love is Letting Go of Fear (1), and his encouragement of insightful picture books by groups of children (see references to Chapter 1), while Shneidman is respected for the many books that he has edited--especially Death: Current Perspectives (2), soon to appear in a third edition, two fine volumes that he has authored--Deaths of Man (3) and Voices of Death (4), and his long service just recently concluded as editor of the journal, Suicide and Life-Threatening Behavior. Some of these two authors' differences in tone, style, and orientation will be evident in the two chapters of this Section.

But one can also discover important dimensions of communality in Chapters 1 and 2. Both authors have adopted insightful ways of taking a new look at very old and very fundamental phenomena of human experience. Both advise that we begin again in our various studies and interactions with a broad vision of the needs of total persons and of joining or the making of social community. In Shneidman's well-known phrase, "death is oxymoronic." So, too, it often seems, is love. Death, grief, and mourning are age-old aspects of human life. So also are estrangement and separation. How can we re-connect with these realities of living and learn to cope with them in more effective ways? Clearly, to do so will depend upon what is best in us, and will require disciplined and creative efforts. In this service, our best teachers will be children, those who are in the midst of trying experiences, and respected professionals like Gerald Jampolsky and Edwin Shneidman.

REFERENCES

1. Jampolsky, G.G. Love is Letting Go of Fear. Millbrae, CA: Celestial Arts, 1979.

2. Shneidman, E.S. (ed.) Death: Current Perspectives. 2nd ed. Palo Alto, CA: Mayfield, 1980.

3. Shneidman, E.S. Deaths of Man. New York: Quadrangle, 1973; Penguin, 1974.

4. Shneidman, E.S. Voices of Death. New York: Harper and Row, 1980; Bantam, 1982.

LOVE IS THE ONLY ANSWER

Gerald G. Jampolsky

One of the very important teachers in my life has been a young girl by the name of Angela that I met in Jacksonville, Florida. She had leukemia and had gone through all the things that leukemic children and adults experience: needles, hair falling out, and the like. And yet she was a shining light. She manifested a philosophy of letting go of the past, of not being attached. Somehow she had turned things around and was able to understand the philosophy that she was really on earth to give love, just to be a neutral vehicle of living in the now.

One day, as I was talking with Angela and interviewing her in front of about 500 physicians and nurses, I spotted the administrator of the hospital in the second row. I had had a brief conversation with him that morning, and he had shared with me some of the problems he was having. The medical department was on his neck because the surgical department had just gotten a large amount of money, and it just seemed to be one thing after another. He was rather depressed and certainly was not looking very happy.

While I was talking to Angela, I saw the administrator and I said, "You know, Angela, you certainly have been my teacher. Perhaps you can also be a teacher for the administrator, that man in the second row who was telling me he had some serious problems today. I don't think there can be any problem more serious than facing a life/death situation, there can be no problem that great. Yet somehow, even at eight years of age you have been able to turn that around. Maybe you could teach the administrator how to do that? What could you say that might be helpful?"

As soon has I had said those words, I was sorry for them because Angela put her face in her hands and I thought, "Gee, this is too serious a question to ask someone who is only eight years old." But all of a sudden she took her hand away, and I could see that smile and the light in her eyes shine. Angela pointed her finger at the administrator and said, "Oh, I know what you could do Mr. Administrator. You could have your nurse go out and buy a feather and come in and tickle him three times a day!"

Well, perhaps that is what we all need: To learn that there is a different way of looking at the world. If we look at the world only with our physical eyes and physical ears, we will often only see a world attacking us. We will be concerned about the future, and we will be concerned about the past. And we will have lots and lots of questions. I can assure you that there are plenty of days when I have doubts in my mind, and I get caught in the past and the future. But when that happens, I remember my dear friend, Angela, with a feather who is tickling me. As a result, I begin to smile and I start to see that situation differently. I hope you can make use of Angela in the same way.

*   *   *

At the Center for Attitudinal Healing we feel very firmly that our reason for being together is not to cure people with catastrophic illness. It is not to do something about something in the future. Rather, it is to experience <u>joining</u> right now, right this instant. What we like to do whether we are having a meeting of children or of adults, or even whether it is a Board meeting, is to start our meetings that way. (Incidentally, it has taken about five years to have a child on the Board. But now I can finally understand the financial report because that child has to be able to understand it.) I would like to suggest that you do that the next time you meet with a group of people. Just hold hands with the person next to you and close your eyes for a few minutes. Let yourself remember that when you leave the meeting, six months later you probably will not remember much of what was said. But you certainly can remember the experience of joining and love that you will have experienced.

I wonder how many people have seen the movie, "E.T.: The Extra-Terrestrial?" I had an unusual experience of seeing that movie. I was lecturing in Seattle and I arrived about 9:00. There was a movie theater right across the street and I had not seen that film, so I was able to go to it. I was sitting on the aisle seat and a woman was sitting next to me with her four-year-old child on her lap. The lights were still on before "E.T." was shown. I said to the little boy, "Gee, you have the softest seat in the house."

He kind of smiled and said, "Yeah, I know." Then he looked at me and said, "You know, mister, I understand a lot of people cry in this movie."

I said, "Well, yeah, I've been told that too."

Then he looked me over and said, "But you're a big man, and big men don't cry, do they?"

I said, "Well, I cry. I cry lots of times when I'm sad. Sometimes I cry when I'm happy."

Then he shook his head, and said, "No, I don't believe that. Big men don't cry." Then the lights went out.

About half way through the movie, I felt someone pulling my arm. This little face looked into mine, and he said, "Hey, mister, you really are crying, aren't you?" Then he wiped a tear away from his eyes and said, "You know, I'm crying too." That was a beautiful experience for me to remind myself that we are really joined. I believe the reason that movie is so popular is that it really emphasizes the fact that minds are joined and that there is something in reality that is past our physical body and our mind, the essence of our spiritual self. I am convinced that this is what really attracts so many people to that wonderful, wonderful, movie. And I felt so blessed to be with this little boy and feel that there is nothing that really separates us. Because when we are working with life and death situations, it is a feeling of <u>separation</u>, it is a feeling of being alone that causes us the greatest distress.

*   *   *

How did so many people all come to be involved in the field of death and dying anyway? I am sure it is not any more accidental than my own history, although our conscious reasons might not be all the same. I did have a conscious reason for going into this field, because I came from a family background where both of my parents have always been very fearful of death and I chose to identify with their fear. So I, too, became very fearful of death. I came from a Jewish background and they had a philosophy that said yesterday was awful, today is horrendous, and tomorrow is going to be worse. When you buy into that kind of philosophy, it is very difficult to experience joy. You spend an awful lot of energy worrying about the future and feeling that you are living in a reality where the past is going to tell you what the future is going to be. And that even makes you run all the more.

In 1975 I felt the the world was attacking me. I had a 20-year marriage that went down the tubes. I had become an alcoholic. And I developed incapacitating back pains. It was about that time that I came across some writings called "A Course in Miracles"(1) three books that began to change my life. These set forth the principles on which the Center for Attitudunal Healing is based. The principles were very simple, even simplistic. They state that there are only two emotions: love, which is our natural inheritance; and fear, which our mind invents. They suggest that it is possible to develop a day-to-day outlook wherein your only goal is to find peace, peace of mind, peace of God. That your only function is to practice forgiveness. And that all you have to do is to listen to an inner voice--whether you want to call that the voice of intuition or your inner gut or the voice of God, I think is not important. But to learn to listen to an inner voice for your directions. And the essence of everything, of course, is <u>letting go of the past</u>.

What happened to me was that I began to experience periods of peace that I did not think possible. For example, I was lecturing in 1975 in the fall of that year at an international conference on cancer prevention in New York City. On the plane going back I was meditating and I seemed to get an inner voice that said within the next five years--it was really kind of a five year plan!--I was to start a Center for Attitudinal Healing. It would be a free center, a center that would have as its first project working with children who were facing catastrophic illness. Later we would work with adults. It would be based on these spiritual principles that there are only two emotions, love and fear, that as we put all of our energy into helping and serving another person we find peace in ourselves. And that age was not a determining factor in telling us who our teachers are. Well that was looking at things 360° differently than I was doing. It had always seemed to me that the older you get the wiser you get, the more maturity meant that you knew better who your enemies were and who you wanted to spend time with. But here were some statements saying that <u>everyone is my teacher</u>.

*   *   *

Let me say a bit about the context for our activities at the Center, and then share some examples of working with both children and adults that I think would be helpful to others since they have been so helpful to me. At our Center on Monday nights and on Thursday nights, if you came there you would find about 25 young adults ages about 15 to 25 meeting together, starting the meetings by joining together and then sharing with each other in an effort to help each other. Not counseling and telling people what to do, but doing one's best not to make judgements, to recognize that unconditional love means not trying to change another person. It is just giving another person full acceptance.

Tuesday at night and during the daytime we have about 20 to 30 adults coming in who have various phases of catastrophic illness. It could be cancer, it could be multiple sclerosis. The only criterion is that of a life-threatening illness.

Every other Wednesday night we have a number of children ages 5 to 12, we have a group of their brothers and sisters, and we have a group of their parents that meet.

On Thursday nights there is also another meeting of young adults. And then we do a lot of work in hospitals. We started a new group this last year which we are very excited about because as I look around this country there are not too many places that meet the needs of these children. I am talking about children whose parents have a catastrophic illness, whose parents may be dying of cancer or multiple sclerosis. What happens to them in our medical system, or our sociological/educational system? To me, they tend to get lost in the cracks. They are not sick enough to call to the attention of the psychologist or the psychiatrist. They are not involved in any kind of religious orientation. And oftentimes they are involved in an atmosphere where the parents are trying to protect them and they are trying to protect their parents. A fascinating thing happens very quickly as you allow them to be in a group and find other kids who are in the same situation: as they begin to help each other, they lose that absorbed self that they were concerned about. The whole aspect of feeling a sense of joining, a sense of oneness, allows them to begin to grasp that sense of inner peace.

*   *   *

Now let me share with you some examples of people whom I have had as teachers. The first child who actually made a transition was a boy named Greg Harrison. He was about 11 years old. I might share with you a dream he had maybe six weeks before he died. It is in the book, There's a Rainbow Behind Every Dark Cloud(2, pp. 78-81). About every medicine imaginable had been given to Greg. The last three drugs that did not work really caused a lot of pain and a lot of side effects. Greg had a dream where he was climbing a ladder and the ladder was going nowhere. He did not know where the ladder was going. Then there was a great big space machine and in the space machine were gremlins trying to throw rocks at him to knock him down the ladder. He drew a picture of

this. I shared with him that as far as I was concerned, whether it is
in life or whether it is in our dreams, we are responsible for the
thoughts that we put in our minds. And it is possible to have all
dreams end in a way that we would like them to end, in a happy dream.
So I asked him, could he draw a picture of how he would like that dream
to really end. He drew a picture of himself and the ladder was ending
in heaven. So there was a place where he was going, there was a
connection. Then he put himself in the space machine and you could see
he had a big smile on his face. And he made the space machine go round
and round and round very fast, so all the gremlins that were throwing
rocks at him fell off. But he was a gentle soul, so he put them in
parachutes so they would not get hurt!

Of course, that was the time when they were considering whether to
use another drug. His parents were putting a lot of pressure on both
Greg and the doctors to have another drug. When they saw his pictures
and when they began to talk about the situation, a decision was made not
to have another drug. And Greg came to the next group meeting saying
that he was not going to have any more drugs, and he knew what that
meant.

The kids in the group, having great candor, said, "Well, what does
it feel like, Greg, to be 11 years old and know that you're going to be
dead in three or four weeks?"

He replied, "Well, you know, how I look at death is that I think
when you die you just discard your body which was never real in the
first place. Then you're in heaven, at one with all souls. And then
sometimes you come back and act as a guardian angel."

Again, here is a young boy who seemed to be acting like a very wise
soul teaching not only me but many, many others another way of looking
at life, another way of looking at death. I have no doubts or question
marks when I pray or when I meditate that Greg is there, assisting me.
And there is no question in my mind that he is a guardian angel for me.

Another important person in my life was a boy named Paul Johansen.
Many people have seen the "60 Minutes" program on which we appeared:
Paul is the boy on that show who had cancer. His story is like this:
Before he went to the doctor he was having some dizziness and some gait
problems. He told his mother that he thought he had a brain tumor. His
mother answered, "Oh, of course that's not what you have!" And the
doctor said, "Of course, that's not what you have." But three months
later that is what he had.

They did a lot of things like surgery and chemotherapy, and he
ended up in the hospital getting worse and worse until he was just skin
and bones. He had already written his will. The doctors, Paul, and his
parents felt that at any moment he might really make his transition.
And then an amazing experience happened. He shared it with me as if he
was not sure whether it was a dream or whether it actually happened. I
think we all have those experiences when we wake in the morning: did
this really happen or was it a dream? In his experience Paul was having
a conversation with God. He told God that he was tired of suffering,

and he did not want to fight it any more. He said that he wanted his
will and God's will to be one. If it was God's will that he was to die,
that was OK, he was going to join Him now. He just wanted God to know
that. But, on the other hand, he told God he felt he still had a lot of
teaching to do. He felt his sister needed some more teaching, as well
as some of the kids at school. And he felt that if he could be given a
little more time, the teaching that he would have to give would be very
helpful. The next morning, without sharing this episode, he asked for
solid food for the first time (he had been on I.V.s all the time)--to
everyone's amazement. I guess about six or eight weeks later he was in
a wheelchair, and after another six weeks he was back in school walking
with a cane.

It was about that time that I was lecturing at Columbia University.
I met his mother there and she shared with me the story about Paul. We
came to be friends, I met Paul, and I began to share with them some of
the principles that we were using at our Center. I think it was about
three months later that I was visiting him. He was depressed and had
some more pain, and I reminded him that at our Center when we are
depressed or unhappy or when we are thinking of death, one of the ways
of getting us out of that situation is finding someone to help, someone
to love. Just the day before I had seen a boy in California named Tony
Bottarini who was perfectly well when all of a sudden they found a lump
in his leg that turned out to be a sarcoma. I wondered if Paul would be
willing to call Tony on the phone and help him. Immediately he said he
would, and I saw right in front of me a boy disappear who was somewhat
pale and had that kind of cloudy feeling over his eyes. In his place,
there was a boy who had joy in his heart and on his face because he was
giving, sharing corny jokes with this kid in California.

Not long thereafter, when I was lecturing in Washington, D.C., a
man by the name of Al Wasserman, who is one of the producers of "60
Minutes", called me and wanted to do a program with us. He asked me
what exciting thing was going on right now. I said the most exciting
thing is that I just came from Connecticut, and there is a kid named
Paul and a kid named Tony. I thought it would be great if people would
see how children could help each other on a love-telephone network. He
agreed. Three days later they were filming it. The amazing thing is
that when that appeared on television--this is almost unbelieveable to
me even as I continue to think about it--60 million people watched that
program. It is almost unbelieveable that that many people can watch a
TV program at one time. The little message that Paul had more teaching
to do was not restricted just to his family or to his school; it was
really to be shared with the world. Paul made a transition on October
17th. His parents called me about three in the morning, my time. And
as I was listening to the news, shaving about six in the morning, the
name of another light in my world was mentioned. Mother Theresa had
been given the Nobel Prize that very day, October 17th. That was a
very, very important day for me.

There also was a boy by the name of Brian who was eight years old.
Brian had a sarcoma and he had a long contact with our Center. About
two months before he died, he had gone to a picnic on Angel Island which
is right across from our Center. There was a balloon lady there named

the Sausalito Balloon Lady. She had hundreds and hundreds of balloons filled with helium. We released them and they went sort of like a rainbow up into the sky. And there was also another man named Nathan who had a lot of different instruments and with whom Brian sang.

I guess it was about a week before Brian died, I was visiting him and his parents, and had taken his sister, who was six years old, for a walk. The parents were very concerned about what was going on in her mind. When we came back I asked her if she could draw a picture. And she drew a picture which told me she was in a very good place. She drew a picture showing her brother with wings on flying up into the sky. Then, because she could not yet write, she dictated to me, and she said, "Heaven is a place where there is no pain. Heaven is a place where there's only happiness because all there is is love and all you spend your time doing is talking with God." Well, this really released an awful lot for the parents.

At twelve noon, about a week later, we were just finishing a staff meeting and I received a phone call from his parents that Brian had just died five minutes earlier, and asking us to come. So Tom Pinkson, a psychologist who works at our Center, and myself cancelled our schedules and went to be with the family. We found that many relatives and friends who were coming in were the distraught ones and it was Brian's parents who were helping those who were visiting with their own peace. I have found very frequently that the parents we work with seem to be able to administer peace to people who are coming in rather than vice versa, that more of the teaching is going the other way. It is an amazing experience to witness.

I remember some of the children in the neighborhood, friends of Brian, how upset they were that maybe they had not visited enough. So what we did was gather them and bring the family together, and the kids in the neighborhood began talking about some of the things. For example, Brian was very angry with a kid across the street one day. The kid did not know about Brian's hair. So Brian said to this kid, "You know, you make me so angry that I just feel like pulling my hair out." Then he pulled his hair out and scared the hell out of the kid! But Brian liked that. It was just neat to be in a place where everyone could be themselves and not have to protect themselves, knowing that it was safe to say whatever was on your mind or in your heart.

Then the parents talked to me and to my colleague and said, "You know, we're not religious. We don't want a religious ceremony, but I have already talked to the minister that has a church around the corner and he has agreed to let us use the church. And I'd like you to administer the ceremony like a celebration of life. But, Jerry, I'd like people to come to that ceremony, and no matter how they come, I'd like them to be able to leave happier than when they came." Quite an assignment, I think, when you are dealing with parents and other children who are coming.

We talked about it and all of a sudden the memory of the picnic that Brian was on came back. We decided it would be great having Nathan who sang songs that Brian loved so much. Then the parents thought of

the Sausalito Balloon Lady, and said, "Wouldn't it be great, if after
the ceremony everyone came out and we could give them a balloon. We
would release those balloons as an extension and as a bridge, a rainbow
bridge to Brian, knowing that in our hearts we would always be joined
with Brian and that there would not be any separation."

Then I thought, how are we going to help these other kids during
the ceremony. All of a sudden it occurred to me that his six-year-old
little sister's drawing would be great help in terms of sharing this.
So, we did this and we had a ceremony that was one of love and of light.
I cannot express to you how good it felt. We have some pictures at our
Center of the balloons going up in the air and the smiles on everyone's
faces, including the parents and the sister (because his sister was the
one that did the countdown). And an amazing thing happened. Usually
when you release balloons they all go in different directions and do not
stay together. But all these balloons stayed together like a rainbow
all the time. They just did not deviate. Afterwards I had so many
parents come up to me and say, "You know, I was very reluctant to come
to the ceremony. And I can't understand how I'm feeling more at peace
now than I did before." How grateful they were!

*   *   *

There is another story I would like to share with you. I was in
Ruth Carter Stapleton's house in Texas about a year ago. I do not like
big books, but I saw a small book and picked it off the shelf before
going to bed. The book was <u>Putting God on the Shelf</u>. It was a remarkable book about a very famous theologian in Switzerland who was 64 and
just about ready to retire. He came across the same kind of problems
that adolescents have and those of us in midlife have. You know, what
are you doing here anyway? And are you doing what you think you are
supposed to do? And as he looked back at his life, he was not sure he
really believed in God although that had been his rhetoric all this
time. He really had never had a spiritual or a real emotional
experience. It had all been an intellectual thing. And he began to
become depressed; he began to think he was a hypocrite. What was he
really doing in life? And he became quite depressed.

It was August and so he decided that he would see a psychiatrist.
But in Switzerland things are the same as in the United States: all
psychiatrists take vacations in August. The theologian could not get an
appointment until September. So he decided to put God up on the shelf,
and he went down to the local pub and began drinking beer with the local
people. A week later, the husband of a woman in his congregation died
suddenly just one block from the pub. They found the theologian and he
went over to be of some assistance. When he saw the husband lying there
dead and the wife crying, he opened his mouth to repeat the rhetoric
that he had used so many times. I think that is not so very different
from what all of us have been caught in who deal with life-threatening
illness, it it? It can be ritualistic. It can be something we have
just read from a book.

As the theologian began to open his mouth to give this rhetoric,
there was a little voice inside that said, "Just think the word

'peace'." So he thought the word "peace" for about a minute, and then he wanted to give his rhetoric. But this process kept going on and on and on, for a full hour. He could not believe it. What he found unbelievable was the peace the he was feeling, like he had never felt before. All of a sudden the woman began to talk to him and said, "I can't understand what's happening to me. My husband is dead in the bed right here, and I'm feeling more peace than I've ever felt in my life." The theologian got rid of his defenses and said, "I'm doing the same thing. I'm feeling more peace than I've ever felt in my life." So he went home, cancelled his appointment with the psychiatrist, and began to listen to that inner voice, to have that inner experience, to know it is not the context or the content of what we relate to another person. Rather it is our spiritual presence, our being, knowing that we are always connected with that person and not just on the physical level. That minds do join; that bodies can never. That there is no separation; there never can be any separation. Until we actually believe that, I think whatever we say will not really work.

I neglected to say earlier that at Greg Harrison's funeral service there were two nurses and one social worker from a large teaching hospital who told me they were quitting. They had what you all know as "burnout." They just could not take working with kids any more, having their hearts so close and all of a sudden having them die. I asked each of them where they were in terms of their own belief systems. Each of them had a belief system that I had up till 1975: that life is finite and when you are dead that is the end of the line, and heaven and hell are right here, and there is nothing afterwards. I think it would be very difficult to really work in this field--in a whole way--feeling like that. That causes a lot of burnout, because your goal is then to keep people alive. Your goal is to take pain away from persons. And that is not what Mother Theresa does.

* * *

Incidentally, I, too, had a miracle experience. In February I was traveling around the world and one of the places at which I was speaking was the Transpersonal Conference in Bombay. I was going to go on to Calcutta knowing that you never know for sure whether Mother Theresa is going to be there. But it happened that the Karmapa died of cancer and she replaced the Karmapa on the program. Since she was there, I was able to get an appointment with her at eight o'clock at the place where she came in late Friday night. Then, since I was the only person that knew her, they asked me if I would drive her to the hotel to give the speech. I thought that was great! Not only did I have a ten-minute interview, but I had another 15 minutes with her in the car taking her to the lecture. One of the things I wanted to ask her--as I have with a number of other people--was whether she would be willing to have an interview where children would be asking the questions about peace. She agreed to do that.

After her lecture, she invited my son and me to travel with her. She was going to Nisek about four and one-half hours away. So we had the rare experience of being in the same car with Mother Theresa from eight in the morning until 4:30 the next morning.   It was a most unusual experience.

As you know, Mother Theresa's goal in working with people is not to have them live longer, but to have them live with dignity.   All she does is something very simple, she just sees the dignity of love in them and gives them love.   Those of us who are caught in the medical model with its goal of taking pain away from people are always sooner or later going to be in distress because there is no way that I know of that you can consistently take pain away from another person.   There is no way of controlling that, of controlling other people--try as you might.   But there is a way of controlling the thoughts in your mind.   Angela was an example, showing that we have the responsibility of changing our thoughts in our minds to having only love thoughts.   For when we have only love thoughts we can only give peace to the person next to us.   You do not even have to say anything, they will know that.   Just being in Mother Theresa's presence, she does not have to say anything, you would not even have had to ever have seen a picture of her, you would feel peace just being in the presence of this woman.

My son had a tape recorder--he is studying for his Ph.D.--and asked her if he could tape the conversations in the car.   One of the things that he asked her that greatly interested me was: if you could pick two things that were the most important to have in a relationship in working with people who are facing a life-threatening illness, what would you say those traits would be?   Without blinking an eye, she immediately answered: meekness and humility.   Two things that are not on the top of the list of most medical schools or most nursing schools--well, at least, during my time.   So, I find myself spending an awful lot of time unlearning a lot of things that I learned in my medical school and in my practice, and recognizing that maybe it is possible to see everyone that we meet as our teacher.   That we are not there to change them, but to give them love.   And we cannot give them consistent love if we are trying to change them in any way.

Mother Theresa also shared a story about a woman that she had recently met in South America who really understood what life was about, what love was about.   She said that this woman, when her child was born, gave her the legal name of "Professor of Love".   Everytime she talked to her child she would have to say, "Professor of Love", knowing that the child was a teacher of love.   Wouldn't it be wonderful if for everyone that comes into our life, today or tomorrow, whether we call them "patient" or not, we could see them as a teacher of love?   Wouldn't we feel differently in terms of our work?

I think we are in this work because we are ready to look at ourselves differently and ready to see life differently.   That is why we are working in this field.   Everyone we see is a teacher.   I still was doing a lot of reading and, I guess, looking for gurus when I first met Mother Theresa in 1977.   It was in Los Angeles and she was going on to Mexico City thereafter.   It was a Fourth of July weekend and I said, "Mother Theresa, would it be all right if I flew with you?   I think just being in your presence would help me."

She said, "Well, I wouldn't object to that."

I thought, "Oh boy, isn't this going to be great!"

She said, "But you did say you wanted to learn something about total surrender, didn't you?"

And I said, "Well, yes, Mother Theresa, that's why I have this appointment."

Then with great gentleness she said, "Dr. Jampolsky, I think you'd learn more about total surrender by finding out how much money it costs to fly from Los Angeles to Mexico City and back, and then giving that money to the poor."

That's a powerful lesson! Because it says, if you want to be healed, the time for healing is right now, the time for healing is giving each other love right here, not seeing any kind of separation, not seeing anyone on the platform knowing anything more than you know. That we are all equal and we are all struggling equally to experience love in a world that is suffering from what might be a terminal illness at this point, a world that is suffering from attack.

*   *   *

Let me give you some other thoughts about people who have helped me. The Shohans have been very much involved with Elizabeth Kubler-Ross and myself. Imagine, if you will, having a 13-year-old daughter who comes down with cancer, and all the things that happen to you in that process, including the miracle of chemotherapy and X-ray therapy. And the doctors saying that the cancer is gone, everything is fine. Then some years later having your younger son come down with a totally unrelated disease, leukemia. And having him die. And one month later having your daughter develop an iatrogenic illness, a disease caused by the X-ray. And having her critically ill in a hospital suffering from incapacitating pain, even though she has been given large amounts of morphine and everything else possible.

They had asked me if I would come to visit them. My colleague, Tom Pinkson, had already been to the hospital. Somehow, the girl was still having excruciating pain. But what I do now before seeing anybody is something totally different than I used to do as a conventional doctor. As a conventional doctor I had a pile of tricks--I am an old geezer, been around a long time, and I pretty much know what I am going to say by the phone conversation and what the voice tells me on the phone. So I have a sense of things in that way. What I am learning to do is to get rid of my bag of tricks and come in with totally empty hands. Before I see someone, I say this little prayer:

We are here only to be truly helpful. We are here to represent Him who set us. We do not have to worry about what to say or what to do because He who sent us will direct us. We are content to be wherever He wishes, knowing He goes there with us. We will be healed as we let Him teach us to heal.

I wanted to quiet myself, to remind myself that my reason for being there was not to take away this girl's pain but to share peace and to be as helpful as I knew how and to be as loving as I knew how. As I began to approach the ward, I heard blood-curdling screams and I felt my stomach go in a knot. I knew I was not ready to go there, so I went back and spent another half hour in quiet. Because I was not ready to experience that; I was identifying with the pain and I did not want to identify with the pain.

Then I went into her room. The daughter was having an I.V. Her father was lying on a cot half asleep and she was screaming bloody murder. I shared with her who I was and asked permission if I could talk with her. In between screams, she said, "No." Then in between screams I said, "Well, would it be all right if I talked with your father." And in between screams, she said, "Yes." And he kind of awakened and I did not know what I was to do. All of a sudden I said, "Why don't you stand right next to her." And I said, "Paul, if you could be any place you wanted to be and you weren't here right now, a place that you have been before and where you could be relaxed, not experiencing and identifying with your daughter's pain, where would it be?"

He said, "Well, it would be on the beach in Hawaii."

So I gave him some suggestions about having him dissociate himself from where he was and having him on the beach in Hawaii. I could see his breathing and his whole countenance change. Then I suggested that everytime he heard his daughter scream he should shower her with love, not identify with the scream but just shower her with love. I saw a person transformed from a man who was in terrible agony and terrible pain to a man who was very peaceful. There were times when I was not that peaceful and I identified with where he was at that point.

Then his daughter got interested in what was happening and said, "I want that to happen to me."

I said, "OK, but my goal here is not to take away your pain. That has to do with you. You have to be responsible. I can give you some door-openings for that, but you are the one that has to deal with that." We tried and it worked for a little bit, but it really did not succeed. Finally it occurred to me to share with her. "You know, I think the real problem that is underlying your pain here is your fear of dying. You don't want to talk about that and you don't want to really believe that you have cancer." Immediately, although I really did not think that she could scream any louder than she was, she went up another 100 decibels, denying this. And then her father began to cry. He began to share with her that, indeed, the doctor and he had talked to her about this, but she did not seem to want to hear it a month before. Indeed, she had a disease that looked as if she was not going to be here that much longer. They had not talked about it because they wanted to protect her. But now he felt that was putting a barrier between them because he really could not be close to her and not share his tears, not share the truth that was in his heart. From all these screams, all of a sudden she began to cry. And they began to talk about a lot of things that they had previously not been able to talk about.

The next day when I came there, she was helping another child in the room next door who had come in with pain. Very remarkable. She went home two days later, and she made her transition, I would guess, about two months later. She died at 9:00 o'clock in the morning, and the parents wanted me to come to the house to do a service that night. By service, I mean a celebration of love. Elizabeth Kubler-Ross did not know that the girl had died. She was supposed to lecture in Oregon and her plane got grounded. So she came to the house not knowing what was happening, and she showed up at this meeting, at this celebration—which was most wonderful.

What has happened to this couple is that they have been a witness to so many people. How can you go on living when you have had this kind of experience? They spend a lot of time at our Center as facilitators for the program that I mentioned earlier: children whose parents have cancer. I have taken them with me on many trips. And two weeks ago Sunday they invited me to their home for another celebration of life. Probably the most gutsy celebration I have ever attended. You see, they have a newborn child! Elizabeth Kubler-Ross was asked to be the god-mother and I was asked to be the godfather. It was a wonderful ceremony of joy. That had to be a pretty gutsy baby coming into the world after that. And they had to be pretty gutsy parents, too, to be able to share their peace. You see, they are at peace because they know that there really is not any separation between themselves and their children, that the essence of their children was present. There is no question mark about that.

I have been struggling to be on a spiritual pathway and I have done my best to let go of any kind of attachment to physical things in my life. I thought I was pretty much there, but during that episode—just before leaving Kamala and her father—I heard a little voice inside me say to give her the gold star that I carried around my neck. Now I have never had any jewelry, but someone who was very significant in my life, named Dr. Helen Schucman, who actually crated the course in miracles gave that to me and she happened to die last February 9th. I was just amazed at a little conversation that my ego had. I was ashamed to really tell people about that conversation, because the ego said, "Well, you know, that's gold, and that's very significant. Why don't you go down to the store and get her another one and then give her that one." And I had this battle going back and forth about what I should do. Finally, I got quieted enough to give it to her, and I felt a tremendous release. Of course, now what is very joyful is that every time I see her mother, she is wearing the star! So one of the concepts at our Center is: giving and receiving are the same in truth, they are always one.

*   *   *

There is still another story I would like to share with you. It is about a boy named <u>Scott</u>. Nothing, I think, upsets a teaching hospital more than having a teenager who is treatable, who has leukemia, but who refuses to come in for treatment. Nothing causes more anguish in social workers, and psychologists, and oncologists, and everyone concerned that that situation. He pressed everyone's button. It got to the point where there was nothing they could do. He also had a juvenile record as big as you could imagine. He was only 16, but he had made enemies of everyone in his life. When no further treatment seemed appropriate he was sent home to die, and somehow his mother called the Center and I was asked to come to see him. He lived in south San Francisco in a rather poor neighborhood. As I was climbing the stairs to his apartment, each wall had holes in it from his fists--to give you some sense of where he was. He wanted to know who I was and obviously was not too happy to see me. It was very clear that I was not to talk to him or ask him any questions, just be. So I spent an hour just being, I did not say anything. I came back the next day and the next day; maybe the fourth day we started talking a little bit.

It was fascinating that each day after that I began to see another person in there. The point came where there were about 20 young people living there. They got his brother out of juvenile hall to give him chemotherapy and shots and things of that sort. And a place where there was great depression and anguish turned into a place where there was great happiness. He told me that what he had decided to do was to forgive everybody. He had all these enemies, one by one, coming back into his life.

Now his father had died a couple of years previously, and somehow the mother had not been able to talk with him about what was going on. She asked me would I do this. I said that I would be a catalyst. I would not do it for her, but I would be glad to do it with her. So one morning when I was there we did this, around such simplistic questions like, Where do you want to be buried?, and things like that. He had answers. He just was waiting for someone to ask him and was trying to protect his mother. He wanted to go back to Ohio and be buried back there. He did not want a funeral service, but he wanted to have a celebration of life service at Fort Mason right next to the Golden Gate Bridge. And he wanted the tape with a great big loudspeaker system, "Free Birds," spread out all over the place. That's what he wanted. He wanted me to conduct it. So we did that and we had about 75 people there. What pleased me most was seeing all the staff there, with forgiveness on both sides.

If we relate this to creativity in death and dying, what you are learning from these examples about creativity has nothing to do with me. It has to do with just being a catalyst to listening. When I was in Australia visiting a hospice last November, I encountered a vivid instance of this. I was introduced to a volunteer as soon as I arrived, and on her tag was her name and one other word that showed me absolutely everything about her. That one word said, "Listener." Can you imagine going into the hospital and seeing the word "Listener?" You would know immediately that the person was a teacher of unconditional love, she was there to listen, not trying to manipulate or to change. As you know, most people who have cancer feel that the social worker is going to come in, or the psychologist, or the psychiatrist--always someone who is going to tell them how they should die or how they should do this or how they should do that. Here is merely the word, "Listener."

*   *   *

We had a boy who was two years old, named <u>Harrison</u>, with cancer of the brain and blind. He came to a Christmas party where my father was. My father was 90 then, blind, and having some problems with his blindness. So this little boy spent a lot of time with my father. But the body did not act like he was blind at all. He was a very happy little boy. My father was not too happy when he came into that room, but he left very happily. To see this little boy as a teacher was a gift for me in helping my father look at things differently. It reminded him that you should just take this instant as the only time there is and not compare yourself with another person.

*   *   *

Next, let me talk about <u>Will</u> <u>Stein</u>. He made the decision himself not to have any more drugs. He lived in Menlo Park and with his parents he started a new center there, in Redwood City actually. About two weeks before he died, I was visiting him and like Paul Johansen he was in a moderate amount of pain and looked pale. I said, "You know, Will, I'm going to be seeing a lot of other 14-year-olds who are facing the same situation that you are facing, and other people at our Center are going to be facing similar problems. I just have a strong feeling that there are things inside you that you haven't shared yet, that could not only be helpful to me, but to other 14-year-olds and other people who are going to be dealing with these situations. Would you consider sharing some of your thoughts on a tape so that this tape could still be here to continue to teach, so that your presence could still be here?"

He had not thought about that before. Again, just like Paul, I could see that gray pallor disappear as he began to talk on the tape. For when you are talking and you are helping another person, all you are thinking about is love. When you are in that instant of only thinking about love, you do not feel pain, you do not feel sickness, you do not think you are a person with cancer--when you are just totally involved and giving. One of the things he said on the tape was that he felt all of us are here to be of service and to love--that is the reason that we are here. He felt that some people are here for short periods of time and some people are here for long periods of time. His assignment, he felt, was to be here for a short period of time, but his assignment was to give love. It is a very moving tape; he called it, "Triumph of Spirit." His parents now live in Houston, Texas, and they have started another center there.

It is interesting how parents have turned these things around as positive experiences. There is a beautiful center in Austin, Texas. It was started by a psychologist, the mother of a teenager who was with us and went back to Austin to die. Last year, they had a conference sponsored by the University of Texas and the Center for Attitudinal Healing in Austin called, "The Transformation of Community." People from all over the city were there to look at principles in attitudinal

healing. They strove to recognize that we can choose to experience love
rather than fear, that we can choose to experience peace rather than
conflict, that we can each instant be a love-finder rather than a
fault-finder, a love-giver rather than a love-seeker, and that we really
are here to teach only love.

                        *   *   *

Next, I would like to share with you some of my experiences in
Atlanta, Georgia. Hugh Prather and I have had an unusual experience of
spending a lot of time there frequently working with parents who have
had children who have been kidnapped and murdered. That is a little
different than cancer because it is sudden. Those parents had every
reason to believe that it is more important to be right than to be
happy. They felt a tremendous amount of justified anger that the police
would not go out and look for their kids because their kids were run-
aways in the first place. They felt that the articles and the news-
papers and the television were saying that the parents were ignorant and
unloving. Supposedly, this was why the children were kidnapped. Also,
the psychologists or physicians who came in seemed to make use of them,
as far as they were concerned, in the media. And they were very
resentful about people who just came and left and got their names in the
paper.

When Hugh and I went to Atlanta we made just one request: that no
one would know we were coming and that there be no press. We did not
know what was going to happen, but we certainly knew how to approach
these parents. Our method was that we did not come there as experts to
tell people what to do. Rather, we came to learn from them--which turns
the whole picture around in a different way. We had the opportunity of
listening, and we were invited back again and again. And it was fascinating to see a transformation take place in these parents.

People cannot be peaceful as long as they have any kind of hate in
their hearts, as long as they have any kind of revenge in their hearts.
What struck me was the strong core of spirituality that most of these
people had most of their lives. There was that initial hate for God-
--how could you do this to me?--that got turned around very rapidly.

I guess it was about six months ago that the kidnappings stopped in
Atlanta. Afterwards, the parents realized that the reason the group was
meeting was that they had something in common. But now there was no
more kidnapping, and it looked like the group was going to fall apart.
One of the fathers had said to me the first time I was there: "Jerry,
how would it feel to you if you had an eight-year-old daughter and you
put her to bed one night and you went there the next morning and she
wasn't there and they found her dead in a river two weeks later? How
would you react?" It was beyond any kind of comprehension that I could
possibly imagine. Well, now this very father said, "You know, we need
to keep together as a group and we need a focus for giving." And the
focus that they picked was battered children. So this group is meeting
now with families of battered children and helping them keep in the
present. They recognize that if they do not keep in the present, they

will fall back and start making judgments about the past and the future. And they want so much to keep their focus right here, right now.

I think that is so important for me and for you. If there is ever to be peace in this world, I think we need to get rid of our fear that we can be attacked. It is possible for us to see the world not as attacking us, but to see it as loving or fearful. Until we come to grips with forgiveness in every part of our own lives as individuals, we cannot really help other people totally. I think it is important really to forgive our parents totally, not partially. That has to be a constant factor. It means forgiving the world and everyone in it and forgiving God. It means taking a leap of faith and trusting God and trusting love.

*   *   *

We have been talking about different ways of looking at death around people who have catastrophic illness. It is also possible to look at planet earth--as many people are doing now--and suggest that the earth is suffering from a catastrophic illness, the possible consequence of which might be global annihilation through nuclear warfare. There are many of us who feel the world is suffering from lack of love.

Although this may seem not in line with our subject, I would like to say a few words about the book, Children as Teachers of Peace (3). Because children in this world today are very worried. They are worried about someone pressing a button and the whole world being destroyed. They are not so concerned about how to help a dying grandmother, but they are concerned with whether they are going to be here. How can something happen as it did in Lebanon? How can something happen in the world? There is a beautiful article in yesterday's Times, "What Can I Tell My Children?" This is written by a Jewish author. Again, the whole aspect of blame.

When I was in Denver about six months ago, Hugh Prather and I were asked to visit a school. The Falkland Islands crisis was going on. So, I asked these kids from six to twelve, "If I could send you to England or if I could send you to Argentina, and you could be a teacher to one of the world's leaders, what would you say to bring peace to this world?"

An eight-year-old said, "Well, you know Jerry, I don't fight very much--sometimes I do--but there would never be a problem so big that we would kill each other, that would result in death. That's what I would tell the big people in the world."

Then an eleven-year-old girl said, "You know, if I was a teacher of the world, to one of the world's leaders, I would say, 'Pretend you're a bird. And you're way up high in the sky looking down. What you would see is that there would be no separation, no division, no differences in colors, and race, and creed. There would only be oneness, and with oneness you wouldn't fight.'"

Let me share with you a few of the comments that the kids made in Children As Teachers of Peace.

"Peace is love between people" (p. 13).

"Peace is friends who get along and make up when they fight" (p. 13).

This is an eight-year-old: "Peace is not fighting because the world may die. Peace begins with me and my mom and dad. How can we teach peace to the world?" (p. 13).

"Peace is when you share a piece of gum with your friend" (p. 13).

"Peace is having your Grandpa come over and spoil you for a couple of days" (p. 17).

One of the ones I like is: "Peace is being quiet alone in a very small bedroom that is messy" (p. 26).

Here is Charlene, age 12: "I think peace is having God holding your hand every step you take...Peace begins with love from God" (p. 33).

Well, a lot of people are wondering if human beings can solve these problems of life and death. They are realizing that maybe that will never happen until we go to a source that is beyond us, until we recognize that our reality is just not limited to a physical reality.

Here's one that many children respond to: "Peace is not getting a divorce in 25 years" (p. 42). You can see how children feel attacked.

"Peace is love that is passed from generation to generation" (p. 48).

After Senator Cranston wrote a four-page document on nuclear warfare, he got something in the mail from little Caitlin which I will read to you. Although he thought his statement was the clearest thing he had ever written, this little letter from Caitlin seemed to be more clear. Many people are very discouraged right now and depressed about the world situation and eventual death.

Dear Senator,
    My brother, my parents and a couple of thousand more are very scared about the arms race.
    My brother is 9 years old. Do you think that it is fair for him to die? If Russia drops a nuclear bomb on us the world will be destroyed along with thousands of people most of whom haven't lived their lives.
    I have a wonderful friend who lives in Vermont. Her name is Erica Tapfer. She is 2½ years old. She moved there last July. I spend sleepless nights afraid of never seeing her before she comes back!
    I would just like to know your opinion. Why do we have to be

bigger than Russia? Why can't we leave each other alone?
I am ten years old and I live in Mendocino, California. You
probably won't pay any attention to me but I would like you to know
one thing. I want to live! I want to be able to grow up and have
a family! I want to have a job and be happy! But all I have to
look forward to is being killed by a nuclear bomb. (p. 83)

Similarly, about four weeks ago I was speaking along with some
children just like these to the Association for Humanistic Psychology.
While I was there, I had dinner with Senator Pell from Rhode Island who
meets with the President once a week, and who was very depressed about
the world situation and what is really happening. I asked him if he
would be interested in meeting with the kids. And he said, "Yes." So
we spent about 40 minutes with them the next day in his chambers. And
although he had grandkids, he was really asking them the questions:
"What do you think about life and death? What do you think about war?
What do you think we should do?" I could see tears come to his eyes.
And I could see a transformation process as he began to listen to
children. In the same way, so many of the kids in this book said,
"Please listen to children." And what we're really talking about is
listening to the child within ourselves, getting rid of the fearful
child within ourselves.

                    *   *   *

In the book, There is a Rainbow Behind Every Dark Cloud(2), there
is a little chapter, "Talking About Death Can Help." "We all found it
helpful to talk about death. It seemed easier to talk about being
afraid of dying with other kids than to talk about it with adults" (p.
82). Lots of times the kids found it easier to talk with the maid who
was swabbing up the floor than it was to talk to the nurse or to the
doctor. "Drawing pictures about what we thought death was like and
talking about the pictures with each other made it less scary to talk
about. It was helpful to find out how other kids looked at death" (p.
82).

There is another chapter, "Praying Can Help." It has a picture of
a boy as an angel going up to heaven and then there is a drawing of a
graveyard and a devil saying, "Lost another one." Then the text says:
"Praying can help. Most of us found that praying was of great help. It
made us not feel alone. It helped us to find faith and hope that we
were safe. When we put everything in God's hands it helped us know that
everything would be okay. It really made the fear go away. I make us
happy and peaceful inside" (P. 89).

Finally, I think the summary that the children wrote is very
appropriate for everyone who works in death education and counseling.

In summary, we think that your mind can do anything. You can
learn to control your mind and decide to be happy 'inside' with a
smiling heart, in spite of what happens to you on the 'outside'.

Whether you are sick or well, when you give help and love to
others, it makes you feel warm and peaceful inside. We learned

that, when you give love, you receive it at the same time.

And letting go of the past and forgiving everyone and every
thing sure helps you not be afraid.

Remember that you are love. So let your love expand and love
yourself and everyone. When you love and really feel joined with
everyone, everything, and with God, you can feel happy and safe
inside.

And don't forget, when you have total Faith, that we are
always connected to each other in love, you will surely find a
rainbow on the other side of any dark cloud (p. 93).

REFERENCES

1. A Course in Miracles. Foundation for Inner Peace, P. O. Box 638, Tiburon, CA 94920.

2. Jampolsky, G.G. & Taylor, P. (eds.) There Is a Rainbow Behind Every Dark Cloud. Millbrae, CA: Celestial Arts, 1978.

3. Jampolsky, G.G. (ed.) Children as Teachers of Peace: By Our Children. Millbrae, CA: Celestial Arts, 1982.

REFLECTIONS ON CONTEMPORARY DEATH

Edwin S. Shneidman

What can we say about death in the contemporary world? First: We live in a death-laden time. In Western history there were other such lugubrious intervals: In the Middle Ages, during the great plagues, during the Napoleonic wars. Philippe Aries, the contemporary French scholar, sketches a millenium of death in his recent encyclopedic The Hour of Our Death(1). But the 20th century has been special; especially lethal. Gil Elliot's book, The Twentieth Century Book of the Dead(2), details the 110 million (!) people killed since 1900 by organized state governments; and the bleedings of World War I and World War II and hundreds of named and unnamed wars and, most awful, the possibility of an atomic bomb disaster.

We live in an oxymoronic century. An oxymoron is any combination of two words which mean the opposite of each other used together for epigrammatic effect. The best known examples of oxymorons in the English language are from Romeo and Juliet, "...Feather of lead, bright smoke, cold fire, sick health" and, of course, "...Parting is such sweet sorrow." I have dwelled on the subject of oxymorons because it so aptly describes death in our time. Death is oxymoronic, a paradox made up of contrasting values, opposite trends, and even contradictory facts.

These are oxymoronic times. At the same time we have created the most exquisitely sophisticated technological procedures for saving one individual's life, we have also created lethal technological devices, of at least equal sophistication, with the capacity of exterminating millions, of expunging cultures, of jeopardizing time itself by not only erasing the present but also threatening the future--what Melville, in White Jacket(3), called "...the terrible combustion of the entire planet." On the one hand, marvelous devices for emergency surgery, kidney dialysis, and organ transplantations promise life; on the other hand, megadeath bombs constantly aimed from above the clouds and beneath the waves threaten death. No one is safe; there is no place to hide as we can see from Kahn's On Thermonuclear War(4), and Lifton's Death in Life(5). There has been no century where so much effort has been put into saving individual lives and increasing the general span of life.

All this gives a psychological and sociological permissiveness--even an urgency--to talk about death. We see this death concern mani-fested in the establishment of hospices, in the activities of clinical thanatologists, in text and other books, in college courses on death education, and in conferences like those sponsored by the Forum for Death Education and Counseling. Death is in the air.

Every once in a while some gifted student of human nature enun-ciates an especially felicitous concept. Weisman's(6) concept of appropriate death belongs, in such company. It is illuminating, elevating, just right, and on the humanitarian side of things. In essence, the basic notion--resting on the assumption that some deaths are better than others, just as some lives are better than others--is that the beneficent thanatologist (physician, psychologist, nurse, or

27

clergyman) should do what he or she can, when interacting with a dying person, to help that person achieve a "good" death.

Weisman defines an appropriate death as "one in which there is reduction of conflict, compatability with the ego ideal, continuity of significant relationships, and consummation of prevailing wishes. In short, an appropriate death is one which a person might choose for himself had he an option. It is not merely conclusive; it is consummatory."

When we speak of a good death, we imply that it is appropriate not only for the decedent, but also for the principal survivors--a death they can "live with." The death is somehow consistent with the decedent's living image. While death itself is the ultimate violation, the nature of death has not violated the image of the person who has died. In James Agee's evocative masterpiece, A Death in the Family(7), Andrew tells Mary that Jay, her husband, died utterly unafraid. He was killed instantly; he was only briefly aware of the danger to him, and then it ended. Andrew says it this way: "Danger made him every inch of the man he was. And the next instant it was all over." His expression at the moment of death was "startled, resolute, and mad as hell. Not one trace of fear or pain." Mary is comforted to hear that her husband died without suffering and without weakness. "Very appropriate," her mother says.

We all recognize that after certain peaks in life's range, there are anticlimatic plateaus where life hangs heavy and time stands still. Shakespeare reminds us in Julius Caesar. "There is a tide in the affairs of man..." An appropriate death comes when one is ready for it. Avery Weisman(8) quotes a doctor's comforting words to a dying patient: "I promise you that you will not die until you're prepared to die."

An appropriate death is appropriate to the individual's time of life, to his or her style of life, to his or her situation in life, to his or her mission (aspiration, goals, wishes) in life; and it is appropriate to the significant others in his or her life. Obviously, what is appropriate differs from person to person: one man's nemesis is another man's passion. Appropriateness has many dimensions, relating, at the least, to the state of one's health, age, competence, energy, prowess, zeal, hope, pain, and investment in his or her post-self. The goals of the clinical thanatologist are to help the dying person have an appropriate death, to help the mourners grieve better, and to support the professional staff in their paradigmatic efforts against death.

How can we prepare for the death of another? One way--admittedly less adequate than one would wish--is to think seriously about the consequences and concomitants of death, specifically about grief and mourning. And that is what I propose to do in this presentation: To ruminate, to verbalize some thoughts on grief and mourning and, at the same time, to build a small bridge to the concept of love.

The famous opening sentence of Sir Francis Bacon's essay "On Marriage"(9) reads as follows: "To love is to give hostages to fortune." It is not because he wrote these words while imprisoned in the Tower of London but rather because of the dire implications of the contents that it is one of the most frightening sentences ever written. To love is to be vulnerable. The alternative is isolation, estrangement, and loneliness. It is both sobering and depressing to reflect upon it. And my own musings lead me to think upon the topic of depression itself.

Depression always has both self-abnegating and wish-for-escape component; in other words, depression has an unspoken subliminal suicidal aspect to it. In this sense, grief then is like a suicidal depression. What makes it different from the ordinary suicidal depression which occurs in the absence of loss is the intense cathexis to the romanticized and elevated memory of the lost person. It is precisely this investment in that memory which serves to keep the grieving person, albeit miserable, alive. Thus, in grief, there is an individual who wishes to die because of the pain of the loss, but who does not commit suicide precisely because of the love for and the fealty to the lost loved person.

Grief is a paradox. Grief is an oxymoron. Grief is the paradigmatic ambivalence. One gradually overcomes grieving as one gradually falls out of intense love with the person who is gone.

When someone commits suicide over the death of another, it is almost always in the brief period after the death--almost like a mutual death pact--before the love-and-loyalty and before the loyalty-through-staying-alive period has begun to occur. Such suicides are committed in the state of initial shock and disorganization, where the loyalty was less than that imagined by outsiders and the felt tie and debt of love is not strong enough to make the survivor, who then quickly committed suicide, fight for a life which, had he or she lived, would have done honor to the individual who had died.

Perhaps the only way to survive another's death is a narcissistic lack of a totally unifying love. The "best" way to survive is, of course, indifference. But that means that there was no love in the first place.

We can now paraphrase Bacon's statement. He said: "To love is to give hostages to fortune." We can now assert: To grieve is to pay ransom to love.

We do not know all we need to know about the process of falling in love. We can now add to our agenda of topics that require further study: We need to know much more about the downward titration of love when the object of that love is forever lost.

In history and in literature, there are examples which illuminate this whole process. Consider: Only a few centuries ago, before satellite communication, before telephones, before telegraphs, and before mail, when someone, a young man for example, left his native village for some new land beyond the seas, it was certain that he would never be seen or heard of again. In such a case, a mother's mourning for her son could have those elements of suicide--ragefulness, hopelessness, depression--transmuted into an ennobling grief that was loyal to the memory of her lost son and eternally hostile to those who had stolen him away--the analog of Death itself.

The introduction of this element of hostility brings us to another, further important point in this argument. When people invented religion, they created special figures to whom they then prayed for their benignant protection from calamity and terror. And by virtue of the fact that they wished to be on their good side, their gods became taboo as the objects of their curses and hostilities, no matter how awful seemed their workings. Credal religious beliefs, by their very nature, interdict blasphemous rage toward the gods, even (perhaps especially) when the loss of death occurs. Death then has to be rationalized. "It is God's will." "This awful event must serve some higher purpose."

So pervasive are these theological constraints in human culture (even for contemporary civilized nonbelievers), that our grief is transmuted from rage (paradigmatically against the gods) to loyalty and fealty to the memory of the love for the lost one, sometimes bordering on veneration. And it is this that keeps us alive until our grief is successfully spent and it is then pointless to commit suicide for a love which has been worn smooth, like a pebble on the shingles of the world, by the daily tides of our emotions. In physical nature, the smoothing of rocks into real pebbles is a process which takes centuries; with humans, in their more finite grief, this process, to be very approximate about it, takes about a year. But of course, the figurative sands of secondary grief stay on the beaches of our psyches all the remainder of our lives.

The phrase, "De mortuis nihil nisi bonum" enjoins us to speak only good of the dead; do not speak ill or hostilely of the dead. In a sense, this is regretable, for it is precisely this interdiction of realistic ambivalence that tends to make our relationship with the dead exaggeratedly univalent and makes the dead person an object of somewhat irrational and worshipful mourning. After all, it would seem to violate the basic rules of fair debate to continue to have a one-sided dialogue with someone who cannot respond. Over the months, as we see that our grief becomes mollified, we can turn more and more to rueful consideration of the dead and deal with those memories in a more realistic and more ambivalent way. When this occurs, the corner has been turned from the acute grief of a venerated being to the realistic, bittersweet mourning of a mere beloved mortal.

All this, above, contrasts in interesting ways with two other human processes relating to mourning: premourning and auto- or self-mourning. Premourning is made up of the droplets of acute grief--the deep and overwhelming sense of loss and abandonment--while the loved person is still alive but obviously dying. Its psychological function would seem to be to inure the potential survivor, step by step--while there is still time--before the loved one's death, so that event itself does not have the shocking effect of a sudden and unexpected catastrophe. Just as there are small deaths--departures, divorces, detachments--so there are also small griefs, rehearsals for the dreaded state to come.

In some senses, premourning--a detachment, a decathexis from a needful dying person--seems to be the most heartless of behaviors, but psychologically we can understand it as a heartful and necessary series of acts in which the potential mourner is seeking to protect himself or herself from unexpected trauma. It is a genuine form of mourning, often reflecting the deepest attachment and not at all implying the disinterest or unconcern which some uninsightful outsiders might misinterpret it to be.

Much of human behavior anticipates some future event. When we cannot prepare ourselves, when we are taken unaware, then we are surprised and unnerved; that is, in part, what shock is. Thus it is not surprising that when we are faced by an inevitable loss (such as the death of a spouse who is dying of cancer), we would both consciously and unconsciously begin gradually to disengage, to deinvest,to inure ourselves to the hammer blows of the real loss before it occurs. That is what premourning is intended to do: to lessen the effects of the actual loss when it finally happens.

In self-mourning (or auto-mourning), the dying individual not only bewails the "naughtment" of the self after death, but, more usually, bemoans the partial losses that are being experienced in the present: inabilities to do things--to run, to walk, even to get out of bed--one could do before the life-threatening illness ravaged the strength and energies. These losses are incapacities: to perform, to cope, to enjoy, to experience in the world. One is gradually reduced to a living brain jailed in a failing body, locked within a bed, usually a hospital bed in a sterile and strange environment, and (whether at home or in the hospital) often a bed of pain.

It is perfectly natural, then, to grieve at the losses that make one less than one used to be. And one is sometimes reduced to poignant wishes like: If only my stomach didn't hurt...If only I could get up and walk across the room...If only I could swallow...If only...

But mostly one grieves about one's memory bank. It is a shame for a mature and learned adult to take the mind's storehouse of memories and wisdom forever from the world, and it is not an act of untoward narcissism for a sensitive individual to grieve over this baleful certainty. Freud(10) said that we cannot truly imagine our own death because, even in the imagining, we always remain as spectators. But that is not the whole story. As we imagine our death--the world without us--we can be spectral spectators (like unseen ghosts), legitimately mourning because the world will somehow be less by virtue of our death.

An elegant, well-educated and thoughtful woman in her fifties, under threat of death from her metastasizing cancer, said the following to me:

> You asked me what I think about my body. I've been proud
> of my body, because it was strong, because I could keep up
> with the children, because I was active. When they were

little, I was as active as they were and could do all the
things they did, and even as they grew older, I was still
able to keep up with them. I was very proud of my body. I
felt it was a good body, a very good body.

And now, I wish I could shed it and get a new one. It's
ruined everything I've had. Up until almost a year ago, I
was such a different person. You just can't imagine. And
now, my body has let me down. And it's not just one or
two parts, it's this complete exhaustion. I just have a
terrible time trying to do anything. I'm just too tired.
I feel totally betrayed. My body has really let me down.

We see here her regrets at what she had once been and her presenti-
ment that she will get even worse, and we see her mourning her own
decline and her eventual death. She said, in another session, that she
was depressed and that part of her depression was related to her contem-
plation of what was happening to her, the further declines in vitality
and energy that were apparently in store for her, and eventually her own
death. She is, in a manner that is quite understandable, premourning
herself. This realistic kind of premourning is psychologically sensible
and is probably in the best interests of overall mental health. Self-
mourning is an important aspect of the "death work" that each terminally
ill person can do in the penultimate days of his or her life.

People uniformly seem to mourn a world that will be without them.
And when you consider it sensibly, to mourn one's own death is a healthy
psychological sign of proper self-respect--which is an integral part of
a healthy personality.

The person who mourns himself or herself has both fantasy and fact
in mind: the comforting fantasy that he or she will be remembered as
someone special--"a perfectly good person with an awful lot to give"--
and the omnipresent fact that we are all biodegradable matter.

The person who mourns most deeply for what might have been is that
individual who knows the dying person best of all--knows intimately not
only his or her own talents but also his or her secret aspirations: the
dying person. And that is why self-mourning can have a special poignant
quality, all the more so because it really cannot be shared.

Self-mourning and denial can, and do, exist in the same dying
person. There are moments of each; not necessarily alternating, not
necessarily existing at the same moment, but present, in turn, during
the days and weeks and months of the dying. The denial that occurs
during self-mourning is in some ways similar to the hallucinated
"assertions" (or re-creations) by the survivor of the recently dead
person--hearing footsteps on the threshold or hearing breathing in the
bed beside you. Those experiences are often a perfectly normal but
nonetheless disturbing part of grief.

Mourning is one of the most profound human experiences that it is
possible to have. Even if it is not possible for an individual to
conceptualize his or her own death, it remains undeniably true that a

person can actually experience the death of another--and to feel the sense of emptiness, loss, fear, and bewilderment.

Grief and mourning can have the effect of reducing a well-functioning child or adult to a howling and bereft person, to an almost animal-like creature. But even at those very same moments, the grief-stricken person displays what is also the most human-like of all characteristics: the need and capacity for social, personal, and loving relationships and bonds. The deep capacity to weep for the loss of a loved one and to continue to treasure the memory of that loss is one of our noblest human traits.

REFERENCES

1. Aries, Philippe. The Hour of Our Death. New York: Random House, 1982.

2. Elliot, Gil. The Twentieth Century Book of the Dead. New York: Random House, 1972.

3. Melville, Herman. White-Jacket or the World in a Man-of-War. Boston: L.C. Page & co., 1892.

4. Kahn, Herman. On Thermonuclear War. New York: Greenwood, 1978.

5. Lifton, Robert Jay. Death in Life. New York: Basic Books, 1967.

6. Weisman, Avery. On Death and Denying: A Psychiatric Study of Terminality. New York: Behavioral Publications, 1972.

7. Agee, James. A Death in the Family. New York: Bantam, 1971.

8. Weisman, Avery. Death and Responsibility: A Psychiatrist's View. Psychiatric Opinion, 1966, 3, 22-26.

9. Bacon, Francis. Of Marriage and Single Life. In Francis Bacon's Essays. New York: E.P. Dutton, 1906, p. 22.

10. Freud, Sigmund. Thoughts for the Time on War and Death. In Collected Papers, edited by James Strachey. 5 vols.; New York: Basic Books, 1959. Vol. IV, pp. 304-305.

SECTION TWO

CREATIVITY IN CONCEPTUAL FRAMEWORKS

SECTION TWO

CREATIVITY IN CONCEPTUAL FRAMEWORKS

One of the most significant ways in which real creativity is expressed by human beings is not in the invention or discovery of wholly new materials, but in the suggestion of innovative ways of understanding and appreciating that which might otherwise have been taken to be well-known and thoroughly familiar. From one point of view, there is nothing new under the sun and there are no new ideas. From another, very ancient perspective, wisdom depends upon recognition of the limitations in human knowledge and of how much we have yet to learn--especially in subjects that seem settled and already mined out. This Section deals with just such creativity, especially as it is applied to established conceptual frameworks or ways of interpreting our world.

In Chapter 3, Kenneth J. Doka looks back over the emergence of the death studies or death awareness movement as a social phenomenon in its own right. Why has the study of "death and dying"--as it is popularly, but perhaps only incompletely called--emerged from the darkness of taboo to the glare of professional and media attention? And why is this broad-spectrum movement very much an experience of the United States and North America more so than elsewhere? Even in the United States, one does not have to claim that popularity, overt attention, or grudging recognition are to be found everywhere among all segments or members of the population. The historical events are sufficiently clear and prominent by now to merit review and--more importantly--reflective analysis. Doka's special measure of creativity lies in the way in which he asks people who read books like the present volume why they are engaged in such behavior, and in the suggestions that he makes for increased personal and social understanding. His work points the way for further research and interpretation.

Quite a different, but no less imaginative, undertaking is attempted by Hannelore Wass in Chapter 4. The broad perspectives of psychoanalysis, social learning theory, and cognitive-developmental theories are familiar to many educators, counselors, and clinicians. So, too, are the general outlines of the ways in which each of these perspectives can be and has been applied to giving an account of children's death-related fears and anxieties. What is original in Wass's chapter is her effort to review these three theories and their application to this particular subject matter in a systematic way. For the most part, they have hitherto been maintained by different proponents or held apart and applied individually only to distinct aspects of these topics. From the work of this chapter, one can see that there is good reason for this. Large-scale theoretical frameworks do not readily converge, and the short phrase "death-related fears and anxieties in childhood" hides a fearsome thicket of complex and intertwined issues. Still, the attempt made by Wass is, as the reader will see, illuminating for both theory and content. Likewise, the dialogue seen here between competing theories and that which they purport to interpret is instructive for adults who hope to help children cope more effectively with death.

Grief and funeral rites constitute another area of human experience in which abound many all-too-familiar concepts and settled patterns. In this volume, the exploration of particular types or dimensions of grief for the sake of their own better understanding is left to the following Section. Here, in Chapters 5 and 6, Nathan R. Kollar and Thomas Attig raise issues concerning conceptual and ethical interpretations of funeral ritual. Ultimately, both authors look towards the articulation of norms for funeral ritual and practice in the future. Kollar approaches that end through a multi-layered analysis of the meaning, goals, and symbols integrated in funeral ritual, while Attig contrasts paternalistic and facilitative models as determinative of an ethic for funeral directors. Both of these chapters thus help to define new and enriched bases for our thinking about this important area of individual and social activity.

THE REDISCOVERY OF DEATH: AN ANALYSIS

OF THE EMERGENCE OF THE DEATH STUDIES MOVEMENT

Kenneth J. Doka

Introduction

The Death Studies movement has come of age. From its early origins in Gorer's provocative essay "The Pornography of Death"(1), and Feifel's 1956 Symposium on Dying and Death for the American Psychological Association(2), through the 1969 publication of Kubler-Ross' On Death and Dying(3), which popularized the field, death studies has been established as a respectable academic undertaking and an emergent profession. There are few professional meetings in the human services, social sciences, and related fields that do not feature sessions or papers on dying and death. Less than a decade ago, Aries observed that:

> It is strange how the human sciences, so outspoken regarding family, work, politics, leisure, religion, and sex, have been so reserved on the subject of death. Scholars have kept silent, acting like the men they are, and like the men they study. Their silence is only a part of the great silence that has settled on the subject of death in the twentieth century.(4)

The silence is now lifting. Even then Aries noted beginnings of the emergence of death studies in psychology, sociology, and in the popular press.

A critical question remains. Why was that silence broken? After decades of denial or omission, what factors contributed to the intense interest in the area that began in the early 1960's? What factors led a society which ignored or suppressed death to now avidly discuss and study it? A taboo does not cease to be a taboo without reason. How was death rediscovered? The question has more than historical importance. Its answer has significant implications for research, education, and counseling as well as for understanding the present directions and challenges facing the death studies movement.

This paper is not the first to speculate on this issue. A number of scholars such as Aries(4,5), Feifel(6,7), Kearl and Harris(8), Klass(9), and Lifton and Olson(10) have offered their insights into the factors that might account for the popularization of death studies. And there have been extensive and systematic attempts to answer this question(11-14).

This paper seeks to review those factors which account for the contemporary emergence of death studies. A possible synthesis of these varying but complementary approaches and a potent explanation of the rise and meaning of the Death Studies Movement* may be found in the work of Pitirim Sorokin. This paper reviews Sorokin's perspective and applies his theories to explain the emergence of the Death Studies Movement. The implications of his theories for the future of death studies can then be considered.

Factors in the Emergency of Death Studies

Four sets of factors have been generally identified as critical to the emergence of death studies and the Death Studies Movement. One factor involves changing demographic considerations. First, death has become increasingly associated with aging. This has impacted on death studies in a number of ways. As the proportion and population of the elderly increased in American society, there has been intensified concern with the myriad problems of the aging. As Neugarten notes:

Increasing numbers of social scientists are focusing attention upon the second half of the life span. In several research centers in the United States, groups of subjects studied since birth are now in their mid-forties, and the developmental psychologists who have been following their progress find themselves studying middle age. Clinical psychologists, whether in hospitals, clinics, or community mental health centers, are spending an increasing proportion of their time with aged clients. Sociologists, as they study new patterns of work and leisure, the effects of increasing numbers of older persons upon the social structure, and the growth of age segregated communities, are perforce turning attention to the field of aging. (15, p. vii)

As social scientists, medical staff, and human service workers have rediscovered aging, they have also rediscovered death. As the proportion of elderly increased, the private problems of elderly individuals, to use Mills'(16) distinction, have become public issues worthy of academic study. It is not surprising that the fields of death studies and gerontology have evidenced concurrent growth and shared membership.

There may be more subtle demographic impacts. Freud(17) hypothesized that anxiety about death affects attitudes toward aging.

---

* "Death studies" in this paper simply refers to the academic study of dying, death and bereavement. The "Death Studies Movement" refers to organized groups which sought to encourage, to disseminate, to apply that research, to advocate for social change in the treatment of the dying, and to train persons in death related counseling and death related education. Such groups would include Ars Moriendi, The Forum for Death Education and Counseling, the Foundation of Thanatology, and Concern for Dying, as well as varied self-help groups.

Perhaps the demographic necessity to confront aging has perforce led to a reconsideration of death. Or as Marshall(13) suggests, perhaps since death, for the most part, is confined to the elderly, it is less threatening. The distance provides space for academic inquiry and public reflection.

A second demographic consideration is that death takes longer. The prolongation of the dying process has been extensively cited as a factor in the emergence of death studies(11-14).

> Recent awareness that death causes human dilemmas has been transformed into a vision of death as the new social problem of our age. (14, p. 12)

This prolongation, particularly in its institutionalized environment, has created strains for family, staff, and institutions; new ethical issues; calls for reform; and experimentation with new forms of care such as the hospice. In addition the development of medical sociology and community psychology has contributed to the rediscovery of death.

A second factor is an historical one. The destruction of Hiroshima on August 6, 1945, created a new historical epoch--the nuclear age. To Lifton, the present preoccupation with death is an artifact of an era of mass and total destruction represented by the nuclear bomb.

> Historical struggles strongly influence the subjects psychologists choose for study. In our time, massive violence and absurd death have made this century one of horror for millions of people. Death has become un-manageable for our culture and for us as individuals. (10, p. 3)

> Finally ever since the day when the age of mathematical physics came to a climax at Alamogordo when a black cloud covered the sun and announced, "I am become Death--the Shatterer of Worlds". There has been a growing pessimism over the future of humanity. (7, p. 354)

The nuclear age threatens almost every mode of symbolic immortality that people use to cope with death. All creations, all descendents, the nature of life itself, are threatened with simultaneous devastation. As Lifton and Olson state:

> The atomic bomb does not merely destroy; it destroys the boundaries of destruction. (10, p. 7)

Or as Fowles(18) writes in aporhisms entitled "Human Dissatisfactions":

> All I love and know may be burnt to death in one small hour.

Death then, as Feifel notes, "is no longer a door but a wall" (7, p. 354).

The nuclear bomb is but a symbol of the mass destruction that Lifton, Olson, Feifel, and others believe lies behind the present preoccupation with death. The violent and highly technological modes of killing employed in myriad wars of this century, the holocaust and the death camps, the starvation and death by violent crime depicted in nightly newscasts, and as Charmaz(14) notes, the sensitization to the possibility of the depletion of biological resources provide humanity with a unique historical problem. To Lifton, death anxiety in the nuclear era is the psychological problem, much as sexual anxiety was the problem in the sexually repressive Victorian age.

Precedent for this view can be found in the late middle ages. The widespread devastation caused by the Bubonic Plague, or "Black Death", created a climate of preoccupation with dying and death evidenced in art, religion, and popular thought(19-21). Contemporary research supporting the historical hypothesis is more ambiguous. Lester(22) found that students were more preoccupied with death in 1970 than similar cohorts studied in 1935. He did not find that global annihilation was mentioned by students as a factor in their concern. Schmitt(23) found that traditional modes of symbolic mortality are clearly evident in a number of segments of the American population and seemingly untroubled by thoughts of planetary holocaust.

Another set of factors are sociological and social-psychological. Social movements frequently accompany larger shifts in values and concurrent social disorganization(24). The 1960's were such an era. The Death Studies Movement was compatible with many of the themes of that era. As Yankelovich(25) characterizes the age, it was the beginning of a new "psychology of entitlement," an era in which various groups translated their desires into a quest for rights. Blacks, Hispanics, Native-Americans, women, elderly, children, and homosexuals began to assert their rights and their dignity. The Death Studies Movement asserted the rights and dignity of the dying.

It was also an era that was characterized by a revolt against a technology deemed dehumanizing. Again, the Death Studies Movement was compatible. It emphasized more humane and personal modes of treating dying and grieving persons; similar to the natural child birth movement, it advocated a 'natural' death. Klass(9) hypothesizes that the popularity of Kubler-Ross' On Death and Dying was precisely due to the fact that it provided a stark contrast of good vs. bad, the simplicity of death in more pastoral times vs. the dehumanization of death due to technology and bureaucratization. This contrast was consentaneous with the mode of the era. As Lofland asserts:

> Finally, it is important to appreciate the degree to which the happy death movements' "critique" of contemporary death attitudes and practices "meshes" with a broader intellectual tradition in the modern United States. I refer to the "humanistic-counterculture" denouncement of modern society in general, which denouncement emphasizes the Western World's dehumanizing, unemotional, technologically dominated, inauthentic, and constricted character. It may be that the movements' "conventional wisdom" draws much of its "believe-

ability" from what it shares with this broader tradition. (12, p. 92)

The emphasis on openness to death and sharing with the dying was in accord with other emergent attitudes(11).

The social disorganization of that time created a crisis for understanding death.

Blows from an impersonal technology are alienating us from traditional moorings, and weakening institutional supports. The consequences are increased loneliness, anxiety, and self-probing. It is an historical phenomenon that consciousness of death becomes more acute during periods of social disorganization, when individual choice tends to replace automatic conformity to consensual values. (6, p. 4)

This technology and bureaucratization created a new crisis. The earlier romantic images of death are clearly ajar from the modern reality of death. Thus there becomes a need to develop new social constructions of the meaning of death (12-13).

Periods of social disorganization are often periods of individualism. And again, this creates a crisis for understanding death. In such an individualized and technological world, the life and the death of any given person can seem to lack significance and meaning.

The clear correspondence between the triumph over death and the triumph of the individual during the late Middle Ages makes one wonder whether a similar--but reverse--situation does not exist today between "the crisis of death" and the crisis of individuality. (21, p. 58)

The Death Studies Movement can be seen as a collective attempt to resolve the crises that emerged in the sixties. Parsons and Lidz(26) have long questioned whether Americans respond to death by denial. Instead, Parsons and Lidz suggest that the basic pattern of response is one of activism. The Death Studies Movement then becomes a collective attempt to "do something about death" in creating new meanings and norms, rearranging institutions, and legislating new laws(12).

Research and scholarship in the general area of aging and death, including efforts such as this book are part of the sense-making and meaning constructing endeavor. (13, p. 194).

A final and significant factor is sociocultural. In a secularized culture, transcendent and theological meanings that assist in confronting death are denied. This theme is exemplified in the work of Ernest Becker(27) and Jacques Choron(28). Their central thesis is that humanity tries to transcend death through symbolic systems such as religion. Secular societies lack such a mechanism; hence denial of death becomes necessary. The incomprehensible death terrorizes dying.

Our lack of meaningful rituals and beliefs makes dying the

more desperate and fearsome and impoverishes life as well.
(10, p. 11)

The Death Studies Movement then is viewed as an attempt to fill this
cultural void(4-5, 8, 12-13, 29). Marshall recognizes this role well:

> It should not be surprising that religion is relatively
> unimportant for many people when they try to make sense
> of death, just as it should not be surprising that many
> other vocabularies seem to be successfully invoked by
> people in legitimating their terminal status passage
> and its end in death. After all, we are by nature sense
> making creatures who abhor meaninglessness...the language
> that people commonly use to legitimate their dying is more
> suited to our secular age precisely because it is secular.
> There is nothing to suggest that secular language works
> any less well than religious language might have worked
> in earlier eras. (13, p. 194)

In a similar way, Kalish equates physicians and death counselors with
priests and death educators with deacons.

> More recently, at least among persons whose opinions reach
> the general public, the ultimate concern is no longer that
> of heavenly immortality, but of a long and healthy life
> on earth, perhaps even of earthy immortality. In that
> case, the priesthood must change. When the God is secular,
> the priesthood must also be secular. (29, p. 74).

The Emergence of Death Studies: A Sorokin Perspective

An integrative and interpretive framework for understanding current
interest in death studies and the emergence of the Death Studies
Movement can be found in the work of Pitirim Sorokin(30-31). Sorokin's
basic presupposition is that all of human culture can be divided into
fundamental societal styles or supersystems. This supersystem is the
"cultural mentality" or the logically integrated nexus underlying all
the specific institutions such as language, religion, art, ethics, and
science. It is the central view of reality, the ultimate exploration of
truth, which will be manifest in all the elements of a given culture.

These styles are of three types. The first is the sensate. In
this system, the ultimate reality is to be found in sense experience.
All social institutions will reflect that central cultural principle.
Science will stress empirical rigor. Art and music will accentuate
sense experience. Even religion will emphasize morality and humanity
rather than more transcendental themes. Contemporary western civilization and the Roman era (from 300 B.C. to 300 A.D.) would be examples
of sensate culture.

A second system is ideational. Here ultimate truth is found in
relationships to some absolute, or God. Reality transcends the senses.
In such a culture the religious institution is primary, and other

institutions such as art and music will reflect transcendental values. Early Greek culture (700-500 B.C.) and the Middle Ages (500-1100 A.D.) would be representative of ideational culture.

A third style is the idealistic supersystem. In this system there is a harmonious synthesis of ideational and sensate values. Sorokin identifies the Greek Civilization (500-300 B.C.) and the Gothic era (1100-1300 A.D.) as representatives of this style. There are also mixed or integrated cultures in which no one theme predominates, such as the later Roman era (300-500 A.D.).

These systems change inevitably and rhythmically. The ultimate cause of change is that integral truth is not identical with any one of these forms but embraces them all. The more a cultural system grows and develops, the more that is left unexplained. As a cultural system develops, cultural items which existed as central elements in the previous super system, become "congeries" or unrelated cultural items in the new supersystem. Eventually there is so much that is unaccounted for that a limit is reached and the direction of change shifts. This point of reformulation and disorganization Sorokin defines as a 'crisis'.

Sorokin's generalizations are sweeping. And as in most macro approaches to theory, there is much to be criticized (32-36). Yet even these critics can recognize that:

> ...even though he may have been wrong on many counts, some of Sorokin's anticipations, written in the 1930's, indeed have a prophetic character. When he wrote about the possible destruction of humankind by the pushing of buttons or about the coming celebrations of hard-core pornography shows an uncanny sense of things to come in the world of the 1970's. (36, p. 469)

Although Sorokin did not deal directly with death[*], one can still apply his theoretical perspective. In a sensate culture, death--the total obliteration of sense experience--becomes the ultimate terror. It is incomprehensible and unexplainable within sensate culture. As such, it may be denied or ignored. But, as the previous analysis indicated, this has become increasingly difficult. Demographic factors and historical circumstance have moved death to the center of consciousness. It will not go away.

Yet, it cannot be explained. Death then becomes representative of what Sorokin would define as the "Crisis of Our Age". Current interest in death studies, the emergence of the Death Studies Movement, and

---

[*]Sorokin does consider the nature of death related themes in ideational and artistic art. (30)

indeed many of the sometimes complementary, sometimes contradictory, movements and emphases of the past two decades can be seen in the Sorokian perspective as symptoms of that crisis. They are attempts to fill a cultural void. Death-related research and the Death Studies Movement can be seen as attempts to construct and reconstruct meanings for death in a culture fervently seeking meaning. In some cases there is the attempt to apply the rigor of empirical science; in other cases this approach is questioned.

> Now the issue is this: why do we assume, as we investigate attitudes toward death, that we have the parameters, the frame of reference for the investigation of death, and that it can only be that which the wheel has turned our way in the last few decades? (37, p. 339)

To Sorokin, current death studies can be seen as meeting a deeply felt cultural need--a need to confront and explain that which cannot be explained in sensate culture. That paradox suggests the paradoxical nature evident in the Death Studies Movement. Symptomatic of times of crisis and disorganization, the meanings constructed and proffered vary; some are sensate, others ideational, still others attempt at synthesis. This is evident in the great variety of work and speculation generated in the past two decades. It is intriguing that the works which have most caught the popular imagination are works that clearly attempt to fill this void. Kubler-Ross(3) offers a carefully constructed and comforting paradigm of dying that urges acceptance and implies spirituality. Moody(38) presents a transcendent vision of death cast in secular terms.

Implications

Sorokin's work suggests many implications for death studies and the Death Studies Movement. First there are implications for research. On a more specific level, there is a need for further study of the factors that are hypothesized as contributors to the emergence of death studies. Research by Lester(22), Schmitt(23), and Kearl and Harris(8) are examples of such creative and timely work. More such research is needed. Secondly, there is a more general need. As Feifel(6) noted, research in this area represents frontiers of science and human experience. Reports of near death experiences(38), post bereavement experiences(39), and other such phenomena are worthy of investigation. At the same time there is a need to recognize cultural strains that press both toward unqualified credence and condescending skepticism. The rigidity of premature closure and the embrace of pseudoscience are both to be avoided. There is research that manages to extend serious study to such topics (e.g., 40).

There are also implications for education. Students may be less concerned with the serious academic study of dying and death and more interested in finding replacements for more traditional, albeit presently abandoned, moorings. Death-related education can help a student encounter his or her own mortality and it may provide exposure to the varieties of answers humans propose in confronting that mortality. Death-related education cannot resolve that crisis.

Counselors, too, ought be aware of this cultural crisis. The temptation to priesthood is strong (cf. 29). Aries points out that:

> A small elite of anthropologists, psychologists, and
> sociologists...propose to reconcile death with happiness. [*]
>
> Death must simply become the discreet but dignified exit
> of a peaceful person from a helpful society that is not
> torn, not even overly upset by the idea of a biological
> transition without significance, without pain or suffering,
> and ultimately without fear. (5, p. 614)

Yet as Feifel notes:

> In this frame, vital grasp of the significance of death
> requires that we see each human being not principally
> as a perceiving consciousness nor as an epistemological
> subject...but as a person, self-aware, involved with
> others, and concerned about salvation. (7, p. 353)

The limits of science and counseling should be recognized. As Feifel warns:

> The current state of knowledge in the field is such that
> the age of prophets is far from over, and we should be
> aware of becoming priests. (7, p. 354)

Feifel's warning is primarily concerned with the premature acceptance of present paradigms and the need for continual mastery of newly developed knowledge; yet his warning also sensitizes to the problem of over-reaching limits.

In similar fashion, Sorokin's work reminds clergy of challenges. Significant numbers of Americans still find solace in religious beliefs, rituals and transcendent modes of immortality(23, 41-42). This is

---

*Lofland(12) also makes this point in characterizing the Death Studies Movement as the "Happy Death Movement".

[*]For example in a recent survey, Blackwell and Tamzyk(41) found that almost 80% of their sample had some concept of life after death and 71% found religious convictions important in dealing with death. Sixty percent found rituals to be helpful. Gallup (42) found that 69% of his sample believed in life after death.

congruent with Sorokins' comment that aspects of one cultural system are
likely to remain as congeries in another even though they are unrelated
to dominant cultural themes. The necessity for death-related education
and preaching within each religious tradition is evident.

Finally, there are implications for the Death Studies Movement.
Death studies, coming from a multidisciplinary root, should do what it

can do within the limits of each discipline. There are numerous strains

within the broader movement to be more. As Sorokin warns:

> When some pseudo religion arises, based upon "science,
> rationality, or reasonable, empirically verified truths,"
> it never gets anywhere, representing at best a third-
> class, vulgarized social and humanitarian philosophy
> or pseudo-science. (31, p. 111)

Secularized and 'scientific' religion has been attempted before under
the guise of social science by Comte(36) and others. Recent attempts
are likely to provide as much succor and be equally shortlived and
unsuccessful. Becker's conclusion is sound advice for a movement like
death studies in a Sorokian "Crisis of Our Age."

> We can conclude that a project as grand as the scientific-
> mythical construction of victory over human limitation is
> not something that can be programmed by science. Even
> more, it comes from the vital energies of masses of men
> sweating within the nightmare of creation--and it is not
> even in man's hand to program. Who knows what form the
> forward momentum of life will take in the time ahead or
> what use it will make of our anguished searching. The
> most anyone of us can seem to do is to fashion something--
> an object or ourselves--and drop it into the confusion,
> make an offering of it, so to speak, to the life force.
> (27, p. 285).

REFERENCES

1. Gorer, Geoffrey. The Pornography of Death. In Death, Grief and Mourning. New York: Doubleday, 1965.

2. Feifel, Herman. The Meaning of Death. New York: McGraw-Hill, 1959.

3. Kubler-Ross, Elizabeth. On Death and Dying. New York: Macmillan, 1969.

4. Aries, Philippe. The Reversal of Death: Changes in Attitudes Toward Death in Western Society. In D. Stannard (ed.), Death in America. Philadelphia: University of Pennsylvania Press, 1975, pp. 134-158.

5. Aries, Philippe. The Hour of Our Death. New York: Random House, 1982.

6. Feifel, Herman. Death in Contemporary America. In New Meanings of Death. New York: McGraw-Hill, 1977, pp. 4-12.

7. Feifel, Herman. Epilogue. In New Meanings of Death. New York: McGraw-Hill, 1977, pp. 351-355.

8. Kearl, Michael, & Harris, Richard. Individualism and the Emerging 'Modern' Ideology of Death. Omega, 1982, 12, 269-280.

9. Klass, Dennis. Elizabeth Kubler-Ross and the Tradition of the Private Sphere: An Analysis of Symbols. Omega, 1982, 12, 241-267.

10. Lifton, Robert Jay, & Olson, Eric. Living and Dying. New York: Bantam, 1974.

11. Wood, Juanita. Death as a 'Now' Issue. Paper presented at the Annual Meeting of the American Sociological Association, August 20-September 3, 1976.

12. Lofland, Lyn. The Craft of Dying. Beverly Hills, CA.: Sage, 1978.

13. Marshall, Voctor. Last Chapters: A Sociology of Aging and Dying. Monterey, CA.: Brooks/Cole, 1980.

14. Charmaz, Kathy. The Social Reality of Death. Reading, MA.: Addison-Wesley, 1980.

15. Neugarten, Bernice (ed.). Middle Age and Aging. Chicago: University of Chicago Press, 1968.

16. Mills, C. Wright. The Sociological Imagination. New York: Oxford University Press, 1959.

17. Freud, Sigmund. Inhibitions, Symptoms and Anxiety. In Standard Edition of Psychological Works, ed. J. Strachey. 21 vols.; London: Hogarth, 1953. Vol. 20.

18. Fowles, John. Human Dissatisfactions. In E. Shneidman (ed.), Death: Current Perspectives. 2nd ed.; Palo Alto, CA: Mayfield, 1980, pp. 3-6.

19. Boase, T.S.R. Death in the Middle Ages: Morality, Judgement and Rememberance. New York: McGraw-Hill, 1972.

20. Tuchman, Barbara. A Distant Mirror: The Calamitous 14th Century. New York: Ballantine, 1978.

21. Aries, Philippe. Western Attitudes Toward Death: From the Middle Ages to the Present. Baltimore: Johns Hopkins University Press, 1974.

22. Lester, Davis. Attitudes Toward Death Today and Thirty-Five Years Ago. Omega, 1971, 2, 168-173.

23. Schmitt, Raymond. Symbolic Immortality in Ordinary Context: Impediments to the Nuclear Age. Omega, 1982, 13, 95-116.

24. Killian, Lewis. Social Movements. In R.E. Faris (ed.), The Handbook of Modern Sociology. Chicago: Rand McNally, 1964.

25. Yankelovich, Daniel. The Psychology of Entitlement. Unpublished paper. New York: Yankelovich, Skelly and White, Inc., 1975.

26. Parsons, Talcott, & Lidz, Victor. Death in American Society. In E. Shneidman (ed.), Essays in Self-Destruction. New York: Aronson, 1967.

27. Becker, Ernst. The Denial of Death. New York: Free Press, 1973.

28. Choron, Jacques. Death and Western Thought. New York: Collier, 1963.

29. Kalish, Richard. Death Education as Deacon. Omega, 1980, 11, 73-83.

30. Sorokin, Pitirim. Social and Cultural Dynamics. New York: American Book Co., 1941.

31. Sorokin, Pitirim. Crisis of Our Age. New York: Dutton, 1941.

32. Martindale, Don. The Nature and Types of Sociological Theory. Boston: Houghton Mifflin, 1960.

33. Timasheff, Nicholas. Sociological Theory: Its Nature and Growth. New York: Random House, 1967.

34. Boskoff, Alvin. Theory in American Sociology: Major Sources and Applications. New York: Crowell, 1969.

35. Mullins, Nicholas. Theories and Theory Groups in Contemporary American Sociology. New York: Harper & Row, 1973.

36. Coser, Lewis. Masters of Sociological Thought: Ideas in Historical and Social Context. 2nd ed.; New York: Harcourt, Brace & Janovich, 1977.

37. Murphy, Gardner. Discussion. In H. Feifel (ed.), The Meaning of Death. New York: McGraw-Hill, 1959, pp. 317-340.

38. Moody, Raymond. Life after Life. Covington, GA.: Mockingbird Books, 1975.

39. Hoyt, Michael. Clinical Notes Regarding the Experiences of 'Presences' in Mourning. Omega, 1980, 11, 105-111.

40. Kastenbaum, Robert (ed.). Between Life and Death. New York: Springer, 1974.

41. Blackwell, Roger & Talarzyk, W. Wayne. American Attitudes Toward Death and Funerals. Columbus, OH.: Report of the Casket Manufacturers Association, 1974.

42. Gallup, George. The Gallup Poll: Public Opinion 1972-1977. Wilmington, DE.: Scholarly Resources, Inc., 1978.

DEATH FEARS AND ANXIETIES IN CHILDREN:

THREE THEORETICAL PERSPECTIVES AND THEIR IMPLICATIONS FOR HELPING

Hannelore Wass

Thus far, it seems that no systematic attempt has been made to examine existing theories of personality, human development, and learning to identify how these theories conceptualize and explain death-related fears or anxieties in children. This paper is an attempt to begin such an examination. Three theories are examined and three points of view that focus on different aspects of children's feelings, perceptions, and behavior are developed from these theories. One objective is to underscore the complexity of the issues that are involved and to assist in interpreting research findings and clinical observations. Another objective is to discover possible convergence of these perspectives, and most importantly, to consider implications for helping children cope with death fears and anxieties suggested by these theoretical perspectives.

The three points of view concerning children's death-related feelings and behaviors are based on: 1) psychoanalytic theory; 2) social learning theory; and 3) cognitive-developmental theory. The first point of view is concerned primarily with the genesis, causes, and nature of feelings related to death derived from the work of Freud and his followers. The second point of view considers a particular process by which children's experiences influence their feelings about death. Albert Bandura's social learning theory provides the basis for this perspective. The third viewpoint focuses on children's thoughts and their interpretations of events and how these thoughts and interpretations influence their feelings about death. This point of view draws heavily on Jean Piaget's theory of cognitive development. There are other theoretical formulations such as Skinner's reinforcement model, humanistic-perceptual theory, transactional theory, and existential psychology not discussed here because of space limitations. It would be worthwhile to examine these theories as well.

Two basic assumptions underlie this discussion:
1. Death-related fears and anxieties are universal.
2. Exaggerated and unrealistic fears and anxieties about death can impede healthy personality development and functioning.

This paper does not focus on the bereaved or the dying child.

Psychoanalytic Theory

Freud believed that all behavior is motivated by physiological drives or energies which are unconscious. All drives can be grouped into two major conflicting ones, the sexual and the destructive. He later termed these Eros, the wish to live and love, and Thanatos, the wish to die or kill. According to Freud, unconscious drives form the basic units of our personality. Of the three levels of consciousness

that comprise the mind, viz., id, ego, and superego, the id is the
largest segment. In it reside not only all drives and unconscious
wishes but also thoughts and feelings that have been repressed but
continue to influence our ideas and behavior. The ego represents our
perceptions, memory, and judgments. The superego or conscience is the
arbiter of morality. Both the id and the superego are seen as cruel and
relentless exerters of pressure. The ego functions as a mediator
between these two powerful forces. Freud believed that the id, ego, and
superego develop sequentially. An infant's mental life consists
entirely of the id. The ego and the superego develop in early childhood
and are fully established by the age of six.

     In psychoanalytic theory, internal conflicts and anxieties are
critical aspects of a person's life, and effective coping with these is
the basic challenge. Death anxieties in children are thought to be
derivatives of other basic anxieties and develop in early life, beginning with birth, which is seen as the origin of anxiety and the first
traumatic event threatening to overwhelm the organism. Others are
separation anxiety with the related fear of object loss and abandonment,
and castration anxiety which involves fears of mutilation and other
punishment or retaliation, fears of aggression, and feelings of guilt--
all related to the development of the superego. The relationships
between these anxieties and death anxiety have been documented in a
number of experimental studies and clinical observations (1-4). Through
children's experiences such as in aggressive action and interaction with
peers in games, and through the media, such as television and books, the
concepts of aggression and death also become linked in actions.

     Viewed from this perspective, the normal young child is apt to
experience an array of basic anxieties all connected in some way with
death. Early childhood is a period in which unconscious wishes, death
anxieties, and internalized demands are pitted against one another in
fierce contest. These internal pressures are believed to terrify and
often overwhelm a child.

     How then can parents and others help the child cope against these
odds? One answer is provided by Bruno Bettelheim, a contemporary
exponent of the psychoanalytic tradition, and a noted educator and
psychotherapist. Using children's literature as an example of one of
today's educative modes, Bettelheim in his book, The Uses of Enchantment
- The Meaning and Importance of Fairytales (5), contends that children's
literature fails to help the child cope with his or her difficult
internal conflicts and anxieties because it is designed for reading
skills or for shallow entertainment. Children's books deny the child's
desperate feelings of loneliness and death anxiety--except for the
fairytales. Bettelheim then illustrates with some 20 tales what he
believes to be the important function of fairytales. Basically he
suggests that beyond stimulating the imagination, the fairytale treats
all the traumatic conflicts that are part of the child's inner world and
thus allows the externalization of the unconscious and repressed
impulses, wishes, and anxieties in open confrontation with external
demands and the feelings they create. By expressing the conflicts, and
by offering solutions, escape, and consolation, the fairytale helps the
child to work through some of these conflicts. In essence, Bettelheim

believes that the fairytale provides for cathartic release of internal pressures and thereby assists the child in regaining some measure of control over them. In effect, fairytales can be therapeutic and enhance healthy emotional growth. This view is supported by other psychoanalysts (6).

These suggestions are particularly significant considering that most of the fairytales Bettelheim has chosen to illustrate his viewpiont (those collected by the Grimm brothers) explicitly describe cruel and sadistic acts including merciless punishment by death. Some writers with psychoanalytic leanings cite evidence suggesting that such offerings by adults can encourage sadistic tendencies in a child (1).

In the ongoing controversy over the effects of television violence, there are those who argue and claim evidence that filmed aggression and violent acts, including murder, not only do not harm young viewers but are actually therapeutic, for the same reasons that Bettelheim finds fairytales to be therapeutic.

We turn to the second theory which is in conflict with the psychoanalytic tradition and its implications for helping children cope with their death-related anxieties.

Social Learning Theory

This theory holds that it is the child's <u>environment</u> that determines the formation, nature, extent, and intensity of death-related fears. Albert Bandura (7) is concerned with specific types of childhood experiences and the ways they influence feelings, thoughts, and behavior. Bandura believes that while human beings do learn as a result of reinforcement, at the same time they learn--often more efficiently-- without it. He disagrees with the psychoanalytic view of persistent internal drives. He asserts simply that diverse behavior is controlled by diverse causes. He asserts that behavior, attitudes, and feelings can be learned <u>without direct experience</u>, merely by <u>observation</u>, a process termed <u>modelling</u>. Various studies support this position. There is a wealth of data on the positive relationship between parents' aggressiveness and that of their children. There are also findings suggesting that teachers, other adults, and peer group leaders serve as models for aggressive behaviors.

Bandura's theory of social learning deals not only with learning through observation of real life models but of <u>symbolic models</u> as well. These include <u>symbols in the physical environment</u>, such as <u>books</u>.

Filmed Violence

Bandura's own early research was concerned with the imitation of filmed aggressive models (8). This work has been pivotal and was followed by numerous studies of the effects of filmed and televised violence on children's behavior. These studies are reviewed elsewhere (9). Although they did not deal with death fears per se, their findings certainly are applicable to this concern. Although not summarily, they basically seem to indicate that filmed or televised violence leads to increased violence in child viewers, thus supporting the social learning view of modeling. If correct, we must conclude that violence in the audiovisual media is harmful and constitutes a negative force in the socialization process.

In social learning theory the influence of models, live or filmed, is not, however, limited to behavior, such as aggressive behavior or prosocial behavior, but to feelings as well. Bandura (7) has noted that many intractable fears arise not from direct personal experiences of an injurious kind but from observing others responding fearfully or being hurt by threatening objects. These premises are important in considering the development of death fears in contemporary children. It can be argues that today's children have fewer direct experiences with death but more indirect experiences with others' attitudes and feelings about death than in the past. We have some specific research data concerning Bandura's assertion. Lester (10) and Lester & Templer (11) have found that children's death fears resemble those of their parents.

Studies of the effects of television violence on children's death fears and attitudes have shown that unusual violence on television and fears shown by victims results in exaggerated death fears in children (12-13). These findings seem to support social learning theory. Some results indicate that prolonged and repeated exposure desensitizes children, causing them to become emotionally indifferent both to the aggressive acts and to the victims (14-15). In any case, the effects on children's feelings were undesirable. Additional studies are needed in this area.

Children's Books

In Bandura's view, words are symbols in the child's physical environment. Records of the written word are an important aspect of a highly developed culture. Our educational system is based on the premise that human learning modifies the learners' understanding and attitudes. Bandura & Mischell (16) reported that reading about the behavior of others is strikingly potent in altering attitudes. Unfortunately, however, there have been no studies to confirm specifically their finding with regard to death fears. There is an extensive, ever-increasing literature of children's books that deals with various aspects of dying, death, and bereavement (17-18) based on the notion that books not only help children to comprehend death but also help them to cope with their death-related fears and reduce these fears by showing how the protagonists cope.

What of the fairytale in social learning theory? It seems obvious that in terms of this theory those fairytales that described sadistic cruelty and murder would be harmful to the child in the same way that live and televised violence has been found to be.

Cognitive-Developmental Theory

The third theory we consider is the Cognitive-Development Theory. Put very briefly, Piaget believes that intellectual development begins at birth with sensorimotor action sequences that form schemata. Through the complementary processes of assimilation and accommodation of experiences, range and complexity of schemata are increased and distorted schemata are corrected. Piaget believes that these processes occur in an orderly sequence. He devoted many years of study to identifying, describing, and elaborating the quality of thoughts, perceptions, and reasoning levels, and their progression. The theory also describes and explains children's misconceptions thus giving us a better understanding of the child's thinking. The usefulness of this theory in understanding children's death-related perceptions and a review of the supporting research literature are discussed elsewhere (9). It would be helpful to review the stages of cognitive development here but that would require too much space. In this discussion, we are concerned with how the child's perceptions and thinking influence his or her feelings about death. From the cognitive-developmental theory we can develop the view that a child's thoughts about death, and a child's interpretation of his or her perception of death are a source of death-related fears. A number of studies and clinical case reports provide evidence in support of this view (1-2, 19-22). I can only give a few illustrations here. The young child's understanding of death as a reversible event can be explained in cognitive-developmental theory by several types of causal thinking processes the child is using in the preoperational period. Three such processes seem particularly relevant here. They are phenomenistic, magical, and psychological causality. Phenomenistic causality refers to the young child's tendency to related causally two events that occur together in time and space. For example, the young child often explains: "Somebody dies because the nurse gives him a pill." Magical thinking refers to the power of people and objects over other people and objects. In magical thinking anything can be explained. There are no surprises. Anything or anybody can cause things to happen to the child. The child, however, also possesses magic powers to protect and to wish things for others. Piaget (23) and others (4, 24) have given clinical case examples of magical thinking that are relevant here. The young child may wish a parent or sibling dead. In the event that a parent or sibling should actually die, the child may believe that he or she caused the death. This would lead not only to guilt but to fears of punishment for such a "wicked" act, as well as a fear of one's own perceived omnipotence. Psychological causality refers to the tendency to perceive a psychological motive as the cause of everything. "People die because they are naughty...", "because they stole some cookies", "because they have done something bad and God kills them", etc.

With respect to the state of being dead, the preoperational child should not be very fearful. After all, at this stage, he or she conceives death to be only temporary. It is, however, perceived to be a restriction, a confinement, a state of not being able to move, of having to sleep. Intense anxieties do develop with the death of someone close, such as a parent, according to some studies (2, 19). These anxieties seem to relate to the loss of the nurturing person and the resulting feeling of having been abandoned, with all the dread and despair this can entail. Studies (22) also show that the child who observes a funeral may become acutely frightened and bewildered. Our funeral practices are inconsistent with the young child's concept of death as a reversible event. For example, since Grandpa is only sleeping, then locking him into a casket and burying him deep in the ground makes it hard for him to get out and come back when he wakes up. Why do people do that? Similarly, the older child at the stage of concrete operations who has come to understand that death is irreversible, whose intellectual interest now centers around the physiological and natural processes of dying, death, and decomposition, is often intensively concerned and fearful of death by murder, mutilation, accident, or disease (1, 21, 25).

A child's capacities always develop in interaction with the environment. Considering the unrealistic portrayal of death on television, one would, from the cognitive point of view, assume that the young child's concept of the reversibility of death is confirmed. This is also true for the fairytale in which the protagonists appear to live "happily ever after". Exposure to television violence should also heighten the older child's fears of being murdered and mutilated, or buried alive.

The child near or at adolescence with full comprehension that death is irreversible, universal, and personal, is believed to experience intense death fears but the young person pushes death and with it the fears out of his mind and treats it as an event in a distant future and turns instead to the more immediate matter of life (20).

The cognitive-developmental point of view has important implications for parents and others who want to help the child. First, it is important not to reinforce the preoperational child's concept that death is reversible as it is done on television, in the fairytale, and often in real life when we believe that we do children a favor by telling them "Daddy has gone on a long trip" or "Grandma will be sleeping for a long, long time". At the same time, the cognitive-developmental perspective suggests that simply telling the child that "dead is dead is dead and means Grandpa isn't ever going to come back" does not enable the child to "grasp" this notion of irreversibility. That capacity develops over a period of time and is made possible by the child's own discovery such as by direct involvement and observation of dead animals, insects, frogs, pets, caterpillars, birds, and pets.

Compromise Instead of Convergence

We have discussed three divergent theories and derived three points of view concerning children's death-related fears and anxieties. Each point of view has implications for helping. The psychoanalytic view assumes that children have intense death-related anxieties that are unconscious and exert pressure for release. Only by confronting and dealing with them cognitively can they be reduced. In contrast, the social learning view suggests that death fears are adopted from live, filmed, or symbolic models that the child observes. To keep these fears at a minimum the child's environment would have to be carefully controlled to avoid models that lead to exaggerated fears. The cognitive-developmental view, in contrast to both others, suggests that not unconscious internal forces nor external models but the child's own perceptions and cognitions are the sources of death-related fears. Since an orderly sequence of cognitive development occurs in interaction with an optimal environment, one would not want to restrict or control it. Theoretically, one could not do much to reduce the child's fears unless the comfort offered lies within the child's cognitive grasp.

This is, of course, an oversimplified account. Obviously, reality is far more complex than this. I would suggest that neither viewpoint is entirely correct or incorrect but that there is some truth in each just as there is in each theory. There are studies supporting each theory. I would suggest that no single theory is capable of explaining the complexities of human functioning including anxieties and fears. I believe each theory and point of view is compromised. I am convinced that the truth is more complex than the conceptual models we devise or even the questions we can think of asking. Still, this is a rather abstract conclusion for the parent, the counselor, or other adult who wants to help the child cope with death-related fears and anxieties. Some position that is more concrete has to be taken. Let me share mine including implications it has for helping the child.

I suggest that psychoanalysts overestimate the amounts and intensities of death-related anxieties raging within the young child. Therefore, the need to work them through vicariously is not so great as they imply, and the dictum is not: "The more monstrous and murderous, the better for the child's emotional health". This means I would not seek out the most murderous and sadistic fairytales for the young child--none of those Bettelheim recommends--but rather those that are more benign. As an intermediator one can soften much of the material. I suggest that social learning theorists overestimate the fear-producing power of environmental models. And we need not begin a futile attempt to screen out all that is potentially fearful in the observable environment of the child This means I would do a careful screening of television programs for violence. I would attempt to help the child see favorable models for their counter-balancing or neutralizing effect. I suggest that cognitive-developmental theorists overestimate the rigidity with which the child is bound up within a given mode of thinking, reasoning, and understanding. This means I would gently explain to the child the facts even if they are outside the child's immediate grasp. I would try to facilitate the child's opportunities to discover death-related phenomena. In any event, I would confront the child as much as I could regarding realistic fears about death.

Summary and Conclusion

In summary, the three theoretical perspectives presented here do not readily converge. Since each has a different focus, it is possible to select from each certain aspects and combine these. The other possibility is that of compromising each theory somewhat, thereby sacrificing purity, but gaining a more realistic view. Many more studies focusing specifically on death-related anxieties and fears in children are needed within the various theoretical frameworks, and, if possible, across such frameworks. Although many studies have been done already, I don't think that we have definitive answers to the question of children's death fears and anxieties.

For parents and other adult helpers, I see three implications that are consistent with any theory, including the three discussed in this paper:

1. Parents and other helpers have critical functions as mediators, clarifyers, reassurers, comforters, carers, and consolers.

2. Parents and other helpers would do well to recognize the uniqueness of the particular child.

3. To help children cope with death fears and anxieties requires the same kinds of characteristics required for other kinds of help: Ability to listen and communicate, an open system of communication, and mutual trust and respect.

References

1. Anthony, S. The discovery of death in childhood and after. New
   York: Basic Books, 1972.

2. Bowlby, J. Separation anxiety. The International Journal of
   Psychoanalysis, 1960, 41, 89-113.

3. Rochlin, G. The dread of abandonment: A contribution to the
   etiology of the loss complex and to depression. The Psychoanalytic Study of the Child. New York: International
   University Press, 1961, 16, 451-470.

4. Wahl, C.W. The fear of death. In H. Feifel (ed) The meaning of
   death. New York: McGraw-Hill, 1959, 16-29.

5. Bettelheim, B. The uses of enchantment - The meaning and importance
   of fairytales. New York: Vintage Books, 1977.

6. Heuscher, J.E. Death in the fairytale. Diseases of the Nervous
   System, 1967, 28, 462-468.

7. Bandura, A. Social learning theory. Englewood Cliffs: N.J.:
   Prentice-Hall, 1977.

8. Bandura, A., Ross, D., & Ross, S.A. Imitation of film-mediated
   aggressive models. Journal of Abnormal and Social Psychology,
   1963, 66, 3-11.

9. Wass, H. & Cason, L. Death anxieties and fears in childhood. In H.
   Wass and C.A. Corr (eds) Childhood and death. New York:
   Hemisphere Publishing Corporation & McGraw-Hill International,
   1984.

10. Lester, D. Relation of fear of death in subjects to fear of death
    in their parents. Psychological Record, 1970, 20, 541-543.

11. Lester, D., & Templer, D.I. Resemblance of parent-child death
    anxiety as a function of age and sex of child. Psychological
    Report, 1972, 31, 750.

12. Gerbner, G. & Gross, L. Living with television: The violence
    profile. Journal of Communications, 1976, 26, 173-194.

13. Noble, G. The effects of different forms of filmed aggression on
    children's constructive and destructive play. Journal of
    Personality and Social Psychology, 1973, 26, 54-59.

14. Cline, V.B., Croft, R.G., & Courrier, S. Desensitization of
    children to television violence. Journal of Personality and
    Social Psychology, 1973, 27, 360-365.

15. Hartman, D.P. Influence of symbolically modelled instrumental
    aggression and pain cues on aggressive behavior. Journal of

Personality and Social Psychology, 1969, 11, 280-288.

16. Bandura, A., & Mischel, M. Modification of self-imposed delay of reward through exposure to live and symbolic models. *Journal of Personality and Social Psychology*, 1965, 2, 698-705.

17. Wass, H., & Shaak, J. Helping children understand death through literature. *Childhood Education*, 1976, 53, 80-85.

18. Wass, H. Books for children: An annotated bibliography. In H. Wass & C.A. Corr (eds) *Helping children cope with death: Guidelines and resources.* New York: Hemisphere Publishing Corporation and McGraw-Hill International, 1982, 95-151.

19. Furman, E. *A child's parent dies.* New Haven: Yale University Press, 1974.

20. Kastenbaum, R. Time and death in adolescence. In H. Feifel (ed) *The meaning of death.* New York: McGraw-Hill, 1959, 99-113.

21. Koocher, G.P. Childhood, death, and cognitive development. *Developmental Psychology*, 1973, 9, 369-375.

22. Nagy, M. The child's theories concerning death. *Journal of Genetic Psychology*, 1973, 73, 3-27.

23. Piaget, J. *The child's conceptions of the world.* C.K. Ogden (ed). Totowa, N.J.: Littlefield, Adams, 1965.

24. Stillion, J. *Death and the sexes: An examination of differential longevity, attitudes, behaviors, and coping skills.* New York: Hemisphere Publishing Corporation and McGraw-Hill International, 1984.

25. Wass, H., & Scott, M. Middle school children's death concepts and concerns. *Middle School Journal*, 1978, 9, 10-12.

TOWARDS UNDERSTANDING FUNERAL RITES

Nathan R. Kollar

All rituals undergo change. This change can be in how we do the ritual or how we understand the ritual we do. In this age of change there are indications that the rituals expressive of both our dying and our death are changing. (1) This paper deals with those rituals associated with the death, burial, and mourning of a human being.

If we wish to understand the change that is occurring in the rituals of death we must answer at least the following: 1) What is/are the meaning(s) of the funeral ritual for the people in attendance? 2) What are the norms that should guide the funeral rituals of the future? If we are to formulate an answer to these questions, we must be aware of the method we use in looking for an answer. This paper examines three concerns in seeking to understand funeral rituals: 1) presuppositions of a method; 2) consequences of these presuppositions; and 3) some questions which must be dealt with in the investigation of funeral rites.

Presuppositions of Method

There are many methods for investigating funeral rituals. We can find excellent psychological, sociological, and anthropological studies (2) about funeral rites. Each of these investigations is valuable. We can only hope for more of them. Yet all these methods, no matter how valid, are reductionistic in nature and seldom attentive to the symbolic nature of the funeral. Using the hard sciences as a model, many methods seek to reduce the entire ritual to one significant focal point of reality in order to understand the whole reality. Yet rituals are people doing and saying things in a patterned way. When one reduces people to only their physical, mental, or social states, one can easily lose perspective on the whole. Somehow this "wholistic" or symbolic perspective must return in the method we use in investigating funeral rituals. Our method for seeking understanding is determinative not only of how we understand (i.e., reductionism vs. wholism) but also of what we can claim it is (i.e., the reality) that we understand. I don't think we have a good wholistic approach for understanding funeral rituals. Thus, this paper is a beginning, a movement "towards" understanding funerals wholistically. Some of the presuppositions of this beginning are the following.

Symbols and Rituals (3)

Symbols are essential for living. Symbols are found in every dimension of human activity and thought. We raise flags, celebrate birthdays, and bury our dead in ways beyond mere bureaucratic efficiency because we are symbol-making creatures. A symbol is a type of sign. A symbol expresses a reality different than itself and makes it present without being totally identical to it. Symbols have an ability to disclose a reality by actually making it present. Thus the flag makes present the nation; the birthday, the life of the person we remember being born. Symbols have a number of characteristics among which are:

their dynamism, community building, their involvement with the whole person, and their expression of many meanings.

Their wholistic nature is evident in the way they affect our minds, will, and heart. Symbols stir up passions. People are willing to die for a flag. Symbols affect our conscious as well as subconscious selves. People involved in a ritual, which is always symbolic, might all at once find themselves crying, ill at ease, or content and satisfied. They have no conscious reason for this feeling but the symbols, the ritual, have affected them at another level of existence, one they may not realize can be touched by symbols.

Symbols are communal. Symbols are primarily agents of unity and convergence. This is seen in the etymology of the word. The symbol is derived from the Greek word sum-ballo, sum-ballein. The verb literally means "thrown together." The noun form refers to a mark or tally used for identification. An object was broken and at a later date joined by the respective holders to form a unity and authenticate their identities. The verb sum in Greek suggests a bringing together. Sum-ballein, therefore, implies assembling or making one what was fractured or divided. A cohesive social group can be recognized by its strong and evident symbols; a weak one has difficulties in agreeing on symbols and their place in communal life. One might reflect upon whether our Western society has weak or strong symbols.

The dynamic aspect of the symbol is seen in the way it brings the other reality into our presence. As with all matters of presence, we may be aware of the other clearly and intensively or weakly and in a sketched-manner. A symbol both hides and reveals. Sometimes it covers one aspect of the reality while uncovering another aspect. This dynamic aspect of symbol enables us to realize that something may be happening in a ritual both when all of our senses are aware of the presence of the reality as well as when, overwhelmed with a personal concern, we are minimally aware of what is happening to us.

We must realize too that symbols always have many meanings. Usually these meanings coalesce around one central or core meaning but when one deals with symbols one deals with a thing, person, or event that is capable of being interpreted in many different ways. The birthday party from the perspective of the mother, the daughter, the daughter's boyfriend, and another male friend are at least four different ways of viewing the same event. These meanings many times depend on the context of the symbol for further specification. When the context is changed usually one changes the meaning of the event for those involved. A funeral ritual celebrated when my parent dies is one event; another funeral celebrated when the president of my school dies is another event. The context is significant for determining the meaning of the event.

Ritual, in general, may be understood as a patterned response of a community and its members to that which is foundational for their life and living. The ritual aspect of the funeral embodies in word and action this foundational or ultimate reality of life and death. Although good ritual always allows room for the spontaneous and individual, its principal thrust depends upon repetition and pattern. This makes ritual a conservative element in any society because it functions as a way of bringing the entire community together: the living and the dead; the present and absent. Rituals come and go but their coming and going are linked to the community and/or culture itself. Construction of rituals is a risky business because they, as with symbols, express and build community. Good ritual can join an individual to a vital community and the basic reality(ies) of life, bad ritual can alienate an individual and destroy his or her relationships to others and to life in general.

That relationship of people we call community is essential to understanding ritual. Ritual builds community as well as presupposes community. Consequently ritual has the ability to reinvoke past emotion, to bind the individual to his or her own past experience, and to bring the members of the group together in a shared experience. A ritual, though essentially repetitious, is able to express and constructively channel the reactions of the mourners. The individual should be able to find his or her own emotions, thoughts, doubts, and convictions resonating within the ritual. The community, on the other hand, should find its deep-felt grief and desire to help engrained in the ritual action. A ritual does not destroy the person. Nor does it take away freedom. Rather it provides a context within which the personal feeling of all the mourners can be expressed, and it offers each individual the occasion to support freely every other individual in this time of crisis.

Although there is always the danger of reductionism, the process of ritual analysis from the perspective of the social sciences is extremely important for understanding ritual action. (4) In a very brief manner I would like to suggest interpretations of ritual from the disciplines of psychology, sociology, and anthropology. These interpretations will allow us to see that ritual studies have a valid and defensible place in those disciplines while providing us with individual disciplinary perspectives of what ritual is.

The work of Erik Erikson (5) provides us with a framework for understanding the psychological dimension of ritual. He offers a chart for understanding ritual based on the conviction that ritual is always interpersonal, repetitive, and adaptive. "...ritualization in man must consist of an agreed upon interplay between at least two persons who repeat it at meaningful intervals and in recurring contexts; and that this interplay should have adaptive value for both participants." (6)

Erikson saw these three conditions present in such diverse situations as when an infant wakes and cries for food, as well as when a country mourns the death of its leader. In each stage of the life cycle a value is introduced through ritual behavior that advances personality development and is reinforced in succeeding stages of adult ritual behavior. The chart below schematizes his correlation of ritual with its appropriate stage of personality development and its inclusion in adult life. His ontogeny of ritualization is shown in Table 1.

Table 1

ONTOGENY OF RITUALIZATION[7]

						Generational Satisfaction
Infancy	Mutuality of Recognition					
Early Childhood		Discrimination of Good and Bad				
Play Age			Dramatic Elaboration			
School Age				Rules of Performance		
Adolescence					Solidarity of Conviction	
Elements in Adult Rituals	Numinous	Judicial	Dramatic	Formal	Ideological	

Let us look at infancy as an example of this ontogeny. The biological and emotional needs of child and mother are the basis of ritual in infancy: the child has to eat and thus needs the mother for that purpose. Consequently both mother and child benefit from the interaction surrounding this eating. Erikson claims that the "greeting" ritual between mother and child effected a "mutuality of recognition" which is the basis for all healthy psychological growth.

In the "greeting" ritual the mother calls the infant by name. The repetition of the name and the care the mother renders the child have a special meaning for the child and the mother. This mutual assignment of special meaning is the ontogenetic source of that pervasive element in human ritualization which is based on mutuality of recognition.

Mutual affirmation is a constitutive element of a healthy human personality and psyche. The repetitive achievement of mutual recognition, positive evaluation, and meaning in and through the "greeting" ritual launches an infant on the path to individual and social maturation. On the other hand, the absence of affirmation and recognition in early infancy will radically injure an infant by "diminishing or extinguishing his or her search for impressions which will verify his or her senses." (8) Once mutual recognition is established, however, the aroused need for stimulation will perdure throughout life as a hunger for new and ever more formalized and extensive ritualization. Once an infant experiences face-to-face recognition, he or she will have a felt need for its fulfillment in a reinforcing repeatable cycle.

This face-to-face mutual affirmation or mutual recognition in infancy pervades all future ritualization. Erikson has identified it as a sense of a hallowed presence or the numinous.(9) On a psychological level, the mutuality of recognition required for emotional growth and stability in infancy finds continued expression and reinforcement in adult religious rituals by this sense of the numinous.

In both the "greeting" ritual of infancy and the adult rituals which convey the mutuality of recognition and the numinous, ritualization reconciles opposites. This can be observed in four areas. First, the mutuality of reciprocal needs in between two unequal organisms and minds, i.e., adult vs. baby; man/woman vs. the "divine." Second, the mutuality of recognition is highly personal yet communal. Each child and mother is unique, yet their behavior is stereotyped. Rituals affect each of the participants differently, yet the ritual is common. Third, the mutuality makes it familiar, yet there is still a sense of surprise when the expectations are fulfilled. An infant still smiles at the repeated games of its mother. A worshiper is still overcome by the "love of God" he or she has experienced in previous religious services.

Finally, ritualization helps to overcome ambivalence. An infant elicits love from its parents, but also feelings of confinement. An infant loves its parents but will eventually experience them as possessive and arbitrary. The "divine" is attractive and loving, yet a reality that can be threatening. There is a growing consensus in the social sciences that the overcoming of ambivalence and the resolution of opposites are not only the effect of ritualization but also its origin and reason for existence. The human person and human society are confronted by oppositions. (10) Ritual is the human vehicle for coping and discovering meaning in this situation. Obviously, the ambivalence of dying and death is most properly dealt with through ritual.

The greeting ritual is one example of a whole process. A process that is necessary for a healthy human life. What I have written suggests the importance of ritual for life. To neglect ritual is to neglect an essential aspect of life itself.

When we look at sociology and anthropology we see that without ritual human community becomes weakened, fragile, and disarrayed. Ritual permeates language, patterns of behavior, and social structure. (11) Let us look at patterns of behavior as demonstrative of the relationship between ritual and human community.

Anthropological and sociological investigations of various communities note a similarity in the way people live. There is, in other words, a consistent, repetitive, or patterned behavior with cultural variations. A behavioral pattern is "nothing other than repetitive human activities that reduce the raw and seemingly random stuff of experience to manageable proportions on both the individual and public social level." (12)

Patterns of behavior control and nourish individual and communal response to life in a threefold way: 1) they foster effective communal communication; 2) they reduce intra-community conflict which could stifle the resolution of binary-oppositions within the community's specific world view; 3) they strengthen group bonding, coherence, and solidarity. (13) Thus patterns of behavior or ritual exercise a significant and central role in all human communities.

Yet care must be taken not to limit our understanding of ritual exclusively to a functional or expressive role in a society. First and foremost, ritual is an articulation. It not only expresses humanness, but is active in bringing it into being. Consequently, it is important to distinguish ritual "before" and "after" formal institutionalization so that neither its articulative nor expressive characteristics are confused, lost, or forgotten.

Before formal institutionalization, rituals are not primarily directed to the establishment of social relations and social structures. Rather, ritual is primarily an acting out of feelings, attitudes, and relationships between members of the social unit, even though social relationships are implicit in all ritual activity. As Susan Langer says:

> Ritual is a symbolic transformation of experiences that no
> other medium can adequately express. Because it springs
> from a primary human need, it is a spontaneous activity,
> that is to say, it arises without intention, without
> adaptation to a conscious purpose; its growth is
> undesigned, its pattern purely natural, however intricate

it may be. (14)

What the ritual process yields, to extend her analysis a little, is not, in the first place, conformity, or social unity, but anchorage, orientation, meaningfulness, and a sense of order.

Ritual not only articulates what it means to be human, but functions to bring about humanness. Ritual is instrumental. It effects a socialization of the individual within the community which provides a sense of orientation and meaningfulness to that person and the community.

I would like to conclude this section on presuppositions by suggesting that religion functions as a means of systematizing the significant rituals and symbols of life. I would define religion as a system of symbols giving unity, meaning, and purpose to human life by being a means of ultimate transformation. (15) All human life, including its rituals, is given orientation and purpose through the individual or society's religious rituals. The schema in Figure 1 both exemplifies this concept of religion and summarizes my presuppositions.

Note:

- Any level of reality can dominate our consciousness at any moment or for a prolonged period of time. e.g., physical pain can orient our whole life.

- The levels, as portrayed, however, suggest a hierarchy of importance. While each is dependent upon the other, each also influences the "shape" of the other.

- The schema portrays a system of interaction is which each is dependent upon the whole and upon each other. A modification of anything in the system changes it. The whole is what exists, the various levels are abstract ways we have for understanding the whole.

- All have a part to play in ritual.

Consequences of These Presuppositions

From the perspective of this schema the goals and orientations of the funeral ritual would be the following. (16)

Physical goals: to cope with the biological needs of all concerned. Thus: 1) removal of the body; and 2) diminishment of physical suffering of the mourners.

Social goals: to cope with death and its effects upon the deceased, mourners, and society in general. To provide group support for the mourners and to express the changing relationships brought about by death. Thus: 1) the funeral should provide an opportunity for the ritual manifestation of shared loss and ritual means by which the support of the community of mourners is conveyed to the bereaved; 2) it should demonstrate social understanding of the relationship of the

Figure 1

SCHEMA OF SYMBOLIC HUMAN INTERACTION

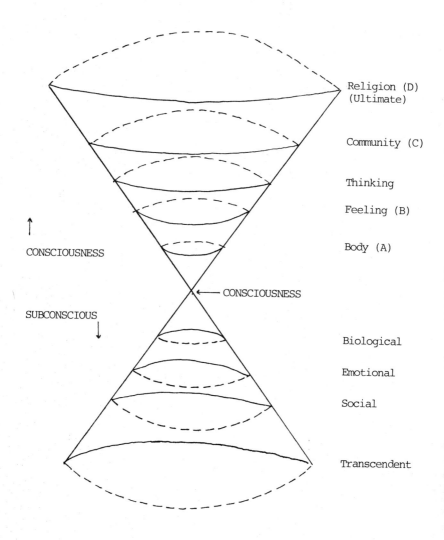

living to those who have died; and 3) it should begin the process of strengthening relational patterns among the living.

Psychological goals: to sanction emotional reorientation of the mourners by helping them accept the reality of the death and their feelings toward the reality. Thus: 1) it should assist in the reinforcement of reality for the bereaved; 2) it should aid in remembering the deceased and begin the recapitulation of the relationship; 3) it should eventuate in the freedom of developing new relational patterns without violation of the integrity of previous relationships with the deceased; and 4) it should offer an opportunity for the release of authentic feelings.

Religious goals: to provide a unified vision of life and death while providing a ritualistic way of enacting that vision. Thus: 1) it should enable mourners to be more meaningfully related to religious resources for coping with suffering; 2) it should offer a perspective(s) on the meaning of life and death in the light of the present crisis; and 3) it should assist the mourners intellectually and emotionally to comprehend more fully human nature as a unity of body and spirit.

The letters A, B, C, and D in the diagram indicate ways in which the dimensions of the funeral can be combined to increase the scope of the function and meaning of the funeral. It should be pointed out that the regular progression described by these expanding segments does not indicate a necessary or inevitable combination. The major purpose of this diagram is to show that the more dimensions a funeral includes, the more potentially effective it will be.

The segment marked "A" represents a funeral which is understood only as a way of disposing of a dead body. This is seldom, except in emergency situations, the sole purpose of a funeral. We usually also find "B" as a part of each funeral. Some simple or more elaborate form of disposition is usually a part of the coping function. Coping, "B", very often also involves some effort to deal with death by seeking a means to revitalize the dead. The form by which this is sought may vary a great deal. It may be the primitive attempt to provide the corpse with all the necessary equipment for living--food, tools, weapons. It may be the more contemporary endeavor to give a corpse the appearance of life in an attempt to cope with the reality of death. It may be the death-defying Christian affirmation of resurrection. In a sense, the whole endeavor to cope with death in the funeral is in some way tied to the question of whether one will or will not face the reality of death.

The segment designated "C" indicates a funeral that deals with three dimensions. It seeks to fulfill its function not only by coping with the realty of death and the disposal of the body but also by offering group participation. The individual mourner does not have to meet death alone but in company with others who share the mourner's loss in part and who support him or her during the period of disorganization due to the impact of death. The group through its rituals, helps to interpret to the mourner something of the meaning of what is taking place. It tries to help the person see that while the one who has died will be missed, life must and can go on. It seeks to convey the possibility for maintaining a relationship to the departed member of the group through memory and commemoration. It strives to respect the separation from the group life which the mourner feels and to smooth the way for his or her return to normal group participation. The funeral, from this perspective, then is a corporate act in which the community seeks to offer its resources to the members with the greatest need in that crisis.

The segment marked "C" also depicts a funeral which includes the group or community showing its understanding of what the mourner is experiencing and its willingness to accept him or her along with all of his or her feelings and questions. In a sense the group through ritual helps the individual free his or her own psychic resources for dealing with the emotions that occur in grieving.

Section "D" indicates a funeral which has its function in four dimensions. The religious dimension places all of the previously described functions into the context of humanity's relationship with the ultimate purposes of life. In a Christian perspective, for instance, the understanding of life and death and the affirmation of the hope for the resurrection become the basis of the coping function. The church, the Christian community, becomes the supportive group which shares the mourner's sorrow and provides him or her with the ritual in which the bereaved is able to find the meanings through which life and death and all that they entail are understood. The reorientation of life now without the presence of the deceased is accomplished in the context of one's relationship with God.

We should note that it is entirely possible, although not likely, that the funeral be limited to one dimension only, A/B/C/D. A funeral might be only a group gathering together to commemorate the death of a member with no religious reference at all. Or a funeral might be only a religious ritual with no awareness of or relevance to the psychological needs of the mourners. Or it may be a group that sees the purpose only in terms of the psychological needs of the mourners as mentioned above. The position being advanced in this paper is that the funeral is most a ritual in direct proportion to the number of dimensions which are involved. The most creative funeral involves all of these dimensions which, as a whole, are normative for authentic funeral rituals.

Necessary Questions for Investigating Funeral Rituals

Although I have presented the purposes and goals of the funeral ritual in a clear and forthright manner, the fact of the matter is that we are not that clear about the actual meaning and function of specific rituals. Methodological problems are present within each of the disciplines that assist us in understanding the funeral. For instance there is not only the difficulty in the interpretation of archeological evidence of death ritual but even more the discovery and the interpret·· ation of more recent rituals and remnants of the funeral rite. Most present day ritual is dependent in one way or another upon primitive Christianity and/or medieval ritual. We have scant evidence of what was done before 1200 A.D. and the manuscripts are most complete and detailed only from the late 15th and early 16th centuries. Thus, from an historical perspective we have a difficulty both with getting our hands on sufficient materials to know what was done and said, as well as knowing the attitude and manner with which rituals were celebrated. (17)

From a psychological perspective, we lack the tools and the occasion to know what is going through people's minds and emotions at the time of the funeral ritual. We can observe what is happening but all the difficulties of scientifically investigating dying and death are found here in the funeral ritual. (18)

Granted, these difficulties I would like to concentrate on formulating a set of questions for ritual studies from the perspective of Victor Turner's work in social anthropology. (19) To understand the funeral ritual we must look at it as a whole, as an interaction of things, sounds, smells, touches, people, emotions, ideas, individuals, and community. This whole is the ritual; not one isolated part of it. Once we make that claim, however, our problem is to understand the ritual as a whole. Many attempts have been made to devise a method which we have seen in the above consequences of our presuppositions. Victor Turner's method is the best for our purposes. It would suggest that we ask the following questions and analyze their answers in order to understand funeral rituals.

1. Can you describe the ritual action as a social drama? Who are the people involved in the drama? Who has the major part(s)? Secondary part(s)? How do they dress? Where does the drama peak? Does it have ritual focus? What things, places, times, objects, words, or books are significant to the carrying out of the drama? How does the drama as a whole reflect the culture of those who act?

2. What is the "structure" and what is the "communitas" present in the act? "Structure" refers to everything in society that defines differences, constrains people's actions, and holds them apart. "Communitas" or "anti-structure" refers to the essential and generic human bond without which there could be no society. Where is the tension between "communitas" and "structure" in the rite? Is it resolved? Are there any consequences of it?

3. What are the ritual symbols? A "ritual symbol" is the smallest unit of ritual behavior--any object, activity, relationship, word, gesture, special arrangement. These ritual symbols have three properties: 1) their multivocality or condensation of many meanings; 2) their power to unify their disparate referents; and 3) their tendency to attract or to absorb meanings around two semantic poles, the one having affective or emotional value and the other pointing to structural or moral norms.

It is in this context of polarity and meaning that we can ask what are the dominant symbols in the ritual? What are the instrumental ones? A "dominant" symbol represents axiomatic values in the society and has this societal referent regardless of its ritual positioning. "Instrumental symbols" are employed to attain the specific goals of a given ritual. Their significance lies in how they are used in the rite.

There are three ways to determine this significance: operationally, positionally, and exegetically. "Operational significance" is discovered by noting who does what. "Positional significance" is acquired as the relationship of one ritual symbol to another or others is determined within the rite. "Exegetical significance" is obtained through verbal explanations as systematic as doctrine or dogma or as subtle as myth. This search for significance and meaning may be formulated in terms of a checklist.

1) What are the explicit and the implicit reasons the rite is performed?

2) What is the form or profile of the rite, how does it flow?

3) Give a detailed description of the site where the rite is celebrated.

4) Give the identity of the subject(s) of the rite.

5) Give the identity of those who are excluded from the rite.

6) What are the things both natural and cultural that are used?

7) Why are they used?

8) What is the relationship of these things among themselves, i.e, what is the structure of the rite?

9) What values are opposed? What values are bound together in structural dyads and triads?

10) What is submerged or present only in veiled form and what is the effect of this concealment?

11) What emotions are portrayed or evoked?

4. Is there some reality to support the ritual action and the ritual intent? Only if there is, will the rite "work" and result in "communitas".

Turner suggests that in the course of ritual action there is an interchange between the affective and the normative poles of meaning of the symbol such that the obligatory is made desirable and the conflict between personal aspiration and social necessity is reduced. This interchange is effected through a dominant symbol that encapsulates the total ritual process to bring the ethical and moral norms into close contact with the strong emotional stimuli. On the other hand, he maintains that rituals break down when the meanings associated with either the affective or normative poles of the dominant symbol no longer obtain, thus making impossible the dynamic exchange in which norms and values become charged with emotional power and basic emotional impulses become disciplined through contact with social values.

If we are to understand the funeral and its possibilities we must be aware of the multidisciplinary dimensions of the funeral as well as have a plan for understanding it as a whole. Turner provides us with a method. I have asked the questions based on Turner. The reader will have to assist me in gathering the answers so all of us can work towards understanding funeral rites.

Endnotes

1. R.M. Harmer. The Place of What Kind of Funeral? <u>Omega</u>, 1971,
<u>2</u>, 150-151.
    Vanderlyn Pine. <u>Caretaker of the Dead: The American Funeral</u>
<u>Director</u>. New York: Irvington Publishers, 1975.
    Robert Fulton. Death and the Funeral in Contemporary Society.
In H. Wass (ed.), <u>Dying: Facing the Facts</u>. New York: McGraw-Hill, 1979.

2. J. Farrell. <u>Inventing the American Way of Death</u>.
Philadelphia: Temple U. Press, 1980.
    R. Huntington, <u>Celebrations of Death: The Anthropology of</u>
<u>Mortuary Science</u>. New York: Cambridge, 1979.
    P.E. Irion. <u>The Funeral: Vestige or Value</u>. Nashville, Tenn.:
1966.

3. In what follows I am dependent upon: E. Cassirer, <u>The</u>
<u>Philosophy of Symbolic Forms</u>, trans. R. Manheim (New Haven: Yale,
1953-57); S. Langer, <u>Philosophy in a New Key</u> New York: Mentor Books,
1948); V.W. Turner, Symbolic Studies, Anthropology Yearbook (1975); W.L.
Brenneman, <u>Spirals: A Study in Symbol, Myth, and Ritual</u> (Washington:
University Press of America, 1978); and reflections on the relationship
between symbol and evil in my unpublished "Evil in the Symbolic Event."

4. An excellent exposition of these levels of ritual action and a
work that I have depended upon for this description is G.S. Worgul, <u>From</u>
<u>Magic to Metaphor</u> (New York: Paulist Press, 1980).

5. Eric Erikson, "The Development of Ritualization", in <u>The</u>
<u>Religious Situation</u> (Boston: Beacon Press, 1968), pp. 711-33, <u>and</u>
<u>Identity Youth and Crisis</u> (New York: W.W. Norton, 1968), pp. 91-141. I
realize there are other ways to interpret and deal with ritual, e.g., S.
Freud, <u>The Interpretation of Dreams</u> (New York: Avon Books, 1965), pp.
155-67.

6. Erikson, "The Development of Ritualization", <u>op. cit.</u>, p. 712.

7. <u>Ibid</u>.

8. <u>Ibid</u>., p. 714.

9. <u>Ibid</u>.

10. Merely cognitive resolution of opposites overlooks the full
dimensions of humanity's capacity to integrate opposing forces. Cf.
Eugene d'Aquili and Charles Laughlin, Jr. The Biopsychological Determinants of Religious Ritual Behavior, <u>Zygon</u>, 1975, <u>10</u>, 41; B. Bro, Man
and the Sacraments, <u>Concilium</u>, 1968, <u>31</u>, 35-50.

11. J.L. Austin, <u>How to do Things with Words</u>. J.O. Urmson (ed.)
(Oxford: Clarendon Press, 1962). A.P. Martinich, Sacraments and Speech
Acts, I" <u>Heythrop Journal</u>. 1975, <u>14</u>. B.R. Brinkman, On Sacramental
Man: Langugage Patterning, <u>Heythrop Journal</u>, 1973, <u>13</u>, 377ff. C.

Crocker, Ritual and the Development of Social Structure: Liminality and Inversion," in J. Shaughnessy, The Roots of Ritual, (Grand Rapids, Michigan: Eerdmans, 1973), 47-86.

12. A. Kavanagh, The Role of Ritual in Personal Development, in The Roots of Ritual, op. cit., p. 153.

13. Ibid., 154.

14. S. Langer, Philosophy in a New Key (New York: Mentor Books, 1948), p. 40.

15. Cf. my "Death, Suffering and Religion," in E. Zimmer and S. Steele (eds.), Selected Proceedings of the National Conference, Forum for Death Education and Counseling, (Lexington, MA.: Ginn Publishers, 1979), pp. 119-27.

16. Much of what follows was inspired by the work of Paul Irion's The Funeral: Vestige or Value? Those familiar with this work will notive my dependence upon his work for the ideas contained here. The orientation, however, is slightly different since I emphasize ritual and wholism.

17. Cf. P. Aries, The Hour of Our Death, (New York: Tandom House, 1982); G. Rowell, The Liturgy of Christian Burial (London: SPCK, 1977); R. Rutherford, The Death of a Christian: The Rite of Funerals (N.Y.: Pueblo Pub., 1980).

18. I have begun to develop a printed questionnaire in an attempt to gain more information about people's expectations of funerals. Anyone interested in it should contact me at St. John Fisher College, Rochester, N.Y.

19. Victor Turner. Dreams, Fields and Metaphors. (Ithaca: Cornell University, 1974); V. Turner, The Ritual Process (Chicago: Aldine Publishers, 1969).

WHOSE GRIEF IS IT ANYWAY?

TOWARDS AN ETHIC FOR FUNERAL DIRECTORS

Thomas Attig

A couple contacts a funeral director and urges him to arrange a quick and simple funeral for a stillborn, just delivered by their young adult, single daughter. They are trying to protect their daughter from a difficult experience which they believe will compound her pain and suffering. They are acting as they believe parents should, inviting the funeral director to do what they hope will be in their daughter's best interests. They make no mention of either acting at her request or with her consent. In short, they are acting paternalistically, and they are asking the funeral director to do the same.

Should the funeral director accede to the parent's wishes? Is there a preferable course of action? More than that, are there profess- ional obligations to the contrary? If there are obligations, what is their ethical foundation? These are the questions I wish to explore on my way toward articulation of an ethic for funeral directors.

The Origin and Plausibility of Paternalism in Funeral Practice

Present day funeral practice is dominated by paternalism due to historical circumstance. It is only since between the two world wars, and especially since the Second World War, that persons have come to rely so heavily upon members of this new profession to guide them through the early days of their grief experiences where once they found their own way. Persons suffering from the distress of bereavement have come to depend upon funeral directors who, they hope, have the knowledge and skills to do what has to be done and to help them to begin to accommodate their losses. Persons, rightfully or wrongly, willingly surrender some of their autonomy in thus seeking help. In turn, funeral directors have come to have authority and power in circumstances where the bereaved are experiencing major changes in their lives and when they are most vulnerable. It is in this historical context that the question arises: What are the rightful limits upon the uses of the knowledge which funeral directors have and of the exercise of the authority and power which have been vested in them? This question is especially important given another disparity in the circumstances, e.g., between the greater and more pressing interests of the bereaved and those of the funeral director. Put in this light, the question becomes: Is paternalism the most respectful response to the vulnerability of grieving persons?

The plausibility of paternalism as a model for the relationship of the funeral director and the bereaved derives in part from its acknowledgement of the disparities in experience, knowledge, and interests just discussed. On the paternalistic model, the idea is that the responsible use of the greater authority is to pursue courses of action which are perceived by the professional to be in the best interests of the bereaved. Because the funeral director's vision of what is best for the bereaved is thought to be clearer, action based on that vision is construed as respectful of the ultimate well-being of the bereaved, independent of considerations of their consent.

The parents in the case outlined above are acting out of their experience within the family where it is only too common and appropriate for parents to act out of their greater experience and knowledge with the heartfelt intent of promoting their children's best interests. Believing that they at least know best to approach a funeral director, they, in turn, place their confidence in his ability to know and do what is best for their daughter during the funeral period.

Rejection of the Paternalistic Model

On my view, the paternalistic model for the relationship of the funeral director and the bereaved should be rejected. To see why, I need only note the non-applicability of the major purported justifications offered in defense of paternalism. Doing so, at least shifts the burden to those who would defend paternalism here to marshall special additional considerations.

First, paternalism is thought justified by its sparing persons significant harm or providing them significant benefits not otherwise or at least as readily obtainable. This is thought to be the principal benefit of the superior knowledge of the professional and the primary motive for seeking professional services. However, authority in the sense of greater technical knowledge simply does not entail authority in the sense of a right to decide in the light of that knowledge, especially when the knowledge does not encompass personal value components in decision-making contexts. Professionals, in this case funeral directors, have only rarely had special training in value choices. Even if they have had some, they likely do not have sufficient knowledge of the personal values of their individual clients to justify the claim to know what is best for them. Furthermore, much of the information about alternative courses of action and possible consequences which they possess can easily be made available to the bereaved. And, as contrasted with much of what can only be done by a physician or a lawyer, many of the actions which can be taken on the basis of information shared by the funeral director can be performed as readily by the bereaved. Thus, the grieving person not only can choose what might be done in terms of his or her personal values but also whether he or she or the funeral director will do it. In this way, the benefits of the chosen course of action may be obtained as readily without paternalistic intervention.

Furthermore, possible involvement by the bereaved is important given that helplessness is a frequent component of the grief experience and a major aspect of personal vulnerability. One of the principal dangers for the bereaved is that their experienced helplessness will be reinforced, that their perceived incapacity will become real and chronic, that unrelieved depression will ensue, and consequently, emotional accommodation to the death, reorientation, and a return to competent human functioning will not be achieved. Failure to acknowledge, or denial of, opportunities for meaningful action feeds, rather than dispels, what temporary incapacity there is in the lives of the bereaved. Thus, paternalism might in fact undermine effective grief work. It would thereby constitute a significant harm to the grieving person and a deprivation of a potentially significant benefit.

Second, paternalism is thought to be defensible and indeed necessary in a professional relationship where a person is incapable of giving a fully free and informed consent. That is, the person is either: a) not "fully free" due to incapacitating psychological disturbance; or b) not capable of appreciating the consequences of available alternatives. In such circumstances, persons are thought not "to be themselves," and their decisions are thought unlikely to reflect their own reasonable desires. While it is true that many grieving persons sense a diminished personal capacity and consequently find it reasonable to consider allowing others to decide for them, it is simply empirically false that the typical grieving person is decisively incapacitated. To be sure, there is emotional turmoil, but it is equivalent neither to compulsion nor to emotional paralysis. Though decision-making might be painful, this is not to say it is impossible, or that unyielding distortion in the vision of one's own best interest is inevitable or even likely. The bereaved are capable of taking in information about alternatives before them, and, when given adequate time, of making decisions which reflect their reasonable desires and express their "true selves." Moreover, delay in the onset of grief work is widely acknowledge as psychologically dangerous in that the chances for restoration of functioning, and with it meaningful living, are diminished significantly if the typical initial shock and numbness of the grief experience are not overcome early. Thus, it is preferable to presume that the bereaved are capable of deciding and giving direction to their own experiences. On this view, survivor resistance to deciding and acting for themselves is seen as part of the problem. Paternalism only exacerbates the problem.

Third, it is thought that the person on behalf of whom action is taken will at some later time come to agree that the paternalistic decision was correct. In part this argument rests on an assumption of temporary incapacity which has already been questioned. It is thought that consent will be won after the fact. In part this seems implausible in the light of the widespread unhappiness with the outcomes of funeral experiences guided by paternalistic principles. This is not to deny that there are many cases where persons express deep appreciation for the services rendered by funeral directors on their behalf. However, it is interesting to wonder how such persons would react were they to be informed that options and alternatives which they did not even know were available to them had been denied them in the name of their best interests. Such circumstances are quite different from those where a parent can say to a child, "See, I told you it was for your own good."

For all of these reasons, the paternalistic model of the relationship of the funeral director to the bereaved should be rejected as indefensible. Consequently, funeral directors have an obligation not to be paternalistic in dealing with the bereaved.

The funeral director approached by the couple in the case outlined above declined to go along with the parents' request. Instead, he insisted that before proceeding with a quick, simple funeral for the stillborn he would have to speak with the daughter who remained in the hospital. He refused to proceed without her informed consent. Thus, he rejected being a party to the parents' paternalism, and he was intent on not approaching the daughter paternalistically. On his view, and I believe the correct view, his first obligation, if he were to remain involved in the case at all, would be to the daughter. It was, after all, primarily her experience and adjustment which were at stake and her vulnerability which called for his respectful professional response. Fortunately, the couple granted his request to meet with their daughter, instead of looking for another funeral director who might well have been willing to act without the daughter's consent. On my view, and his, the latter would constitute professional malpractice.

Toward a More Plausible Model

If funeral directors ought not to be paternalistic, how then ought they to proceed in their interactions with those they serve? The rejection of paternalism as a model for the central relationship in the funeral context leaves us with the task of articulating an alternative and more acceptable model on the basis of which positive obligations of funeral directors may be defined. Given that the disparities in experience, knowledge, and interest remain, what is an alternative and more respectful response to the vulnerability of the bereaved person?

I believe the preferable model for the relationship is that found frequently in such professions as social work, counseling, therapy, and education. In all of these there is acknowledgement of disparities in experience and knowledge between professionals and those they serve. The difference is in an alternative view of what ought rightfully to be done in the light of that disparity to promote the interests of clients. Professional expertise is to be used to enable clients to decide and function more responsibly and effectively, thereby giving direction to their own lives in terms of their own values. Whereas on the paternalistic model the funeral director's vision of the interests of the bereaved governs, on the alternative model the grieving persons' own vision governs. This is so even when persons, in full knowledge of available alternatives, choose to have the funeral directors do things for them. They are then at least assuming more responsibility in and exercising more control over the course of their own experience though informed consent than on the paternalistic model. To be sure, it is hoped that, optimally, persons will be able to decide and act creatively even in the most difficult of circumstances. For lack of a better term, let us call the role of the professional in thus encouraging, developing, enhancing, and supporting client independence that of facilitator.

Ethics for Funeral Directors on the Facilitator Model

What are the primary considerations which make this facilitator model for the relationship of the funeral director and the bereaved morally preferable? Earlier remarks concerning issues of helplessness and control in the lives of grieving persons argue strongly that facilitation of their functioning as decision-makers and as actors rather than as spectators is more directly responsive to the psychological needs of the bereaved and, consequently, more likely conducive to personal well-being. The major tasks of grief work are directly addressed from the beginning rather than being delayed or postponed. These tasks include: 1) acknowledgement of a significantly transformed reality; 2) achievement of emotional accommodation to the death through the experience and expression of emotion; 3) saying goodbye; 4) reorientation within the transformed world of everyday living including reintegration into the community; and 5) recovery of competent and meaningful human functioning. At least as important, and perhaps more so, are considerations of respect for grieving persons as autonomous agents. On the facilitator model, they are presumed to be competent. The grieving persons' vision of their best interest, a vision defined in terms of their own values--however inarticulate and ill-defined it may be at the beginning of the interaction--takes precedence over the vision of the funeral director as grieving persons are invited and encouraged in giving direction to their own grief experiences.

What, then, are the professional obligations of funeral directors on the facilitator model? Helplessness can be overcome and modes of meaningful functioning defined and executed only if the means of doing so are provided. Respect for the autonomy of persons requires minimally that there be no unnecessary impeding of their decision-making or autonomous functioning on the basis of the decisions they reach. Thus, there is a primary obligation, on both counts, to provide the bereaved with information necessary to informed decision-making concerning their own lives. Funeral directors must be trustworthy in their handling of vitally important information bearing directly and often profoundly on the experience and well-being of the bereaved. Obviously, this requires honesty as against deceitfulness, but it also requires candor. This obligation to candor requires that funeral directors not only respond truthfully to client questions and initiatives but also that they fully disclose rather than withhold information about alternatives of which the typical grieving person is ignorant. It is professionally irresponsible to wait for the bereaved to take the initiative in proposing alternatives and possible involvements in the events of the funeral period when they are largely ignorant of the very possibility of taking such initiative. For example, it is commonly presumed that only funeral directors can sign for and remove a body from a hospital or nursing home. In fact, many funeral directors and medical professionals insist that this is so. There is a professional obligation to inform bereaved persons that there are no such regulations, that the remains belong to the survivors, and that survivors may claim and transport the dead themselves. For another example, it is rare for anyone other than the funeral director to close a casket, and this is most frequently done out of the view of the bereaved. There is a professional obligation to inform bereaved persons that they may choose to close the casket themselves, or at least to be present when it is done. Persons must be informed in general that they are welcome to perform any number of other such tasks themselves if they choose, including participating in preparation of the body (e.g., dressing the body or doing the hair), participating in funeral services (e.g., giving a eulogy or otherwise expressing themselves to others in attendance), or aiding in the final disposition (e.g., helping in transporting the body or helping in the actual burial). Once the general point is made that initiative is welcome, the

range of possible involvements is limited only rarely by official
regulation. To be sure, to insist upon involvement would be paternalistic in its own way. The major professional obligation is, rather, to
make it transparent to survivors that they are free to choose to have
funeral and grief experiences on their own terms. The point is to put
grieving persons in the position where they can on the basis of adequate
information say, "Given what I now know about the alternatives, do this
for me, and I'd like to do this for myself."

Beyond obligations having to do with their knowledge of options
and opportunities available in the funeral period, funeral directors are
obligated to develop and sustain competencies which are essential in
providing services to the bereaved. Funeral directors would hardly be
worthy of trust: a) if they were not technically competent in performing
professional services such as embalming and preparation of the body when
that is requested or in seeing to it that state and local regulations
are adhered to; or b) if they were not knowledgeable about the contours
of the grief experience upon which their actions have such an important
impact. Among other things, this entails that funeral directors must
be competent in explaining the nature of the likely consequences of the
bereaved choosing one alternative over another. Thus, for example, the
common practice in some funeral homes of maintaining that a body,
perhaps that of an accident victim, is simply "not viewable", or of
allowing at most a single survivor to decide whether a body can be
viewed by other survivors, must be rejected. Rather, funeral directors
must cultivate abilities to explain what viewing such a body might be
like as well as the possible consequences of seeing or not seeing it.
They are obligated to develop and be diligent in the use of the skills
which are essential in supporting persons in making difficult decisions,
in experiencing and expressing emotions in turmoil, in confronting and
coming to terms with a transformed and difficult reality, and in carrying out courses of action which they have decided are in their own best
interests.

Conclusion

I would like to conclude this paper with an account of the events
following the initial meeting of the funeral director with the couple
who wished to have a quick and simple funeral to spare their daughter
unnecessary anguish following the birth of a stillborn. The case
provides clear illustration of responsible professional action on the
facilitator model.

Having obtained the couple's approval, the funeral director met
with the young woman and explained who he was, how he had been approached by her parents, what they had proposed doing, and why he had
thought it important to speak with her. It was her experience, he said,
and he wanted to know what her wishes were before proceeding. He
indicated that he could do as the parents requested provided he knew
that was what she really wanted. He invoked a principle of deferred
judgement in: a) telling her what decisions had to be made before he
could proceed; but b) insisting that she not give her answers until he
returned the following day when she had had time to weigh the alternatives. Among the decisions which he suggested were hers and non one

else's to make were the following: 1) Was there to be a funeral at all?
2) If so, did she want her parents to pay for it? 3) Had she seen, or
did she want to see, the baby? 4) Did she want to be there for the
funeral or not? If so, he could wait until she was able to leave the
hospital. 5) Had she named the baby, and if not, did she want to? 6)
Did she want the father to know of the birth of the baby, and did she
want the father's name to be entered on the death certificate? 7) How,
if at all, did she want to go about selecting a casket? 8) Did she
want a minister or not? The session in which these questions were posed
was not an easy one, but there was no pressing for decisions on the
spot. The funeral director made it clear that he thought she was
entitled to the option of deciding for herself what direction her
experience during the funeral period would take and what actions she
would take as against anyone else. It was, after all, her misfortune,
her experience, her pain, and her suffering. The funeral director also
knew that the principal of deferred judgement which he invoked allows
persons to seriously consider alternatives to the initial impulse to
retreat from painful decisions and involvements. Given time, he has
discovered, persons will more frequently choose to confront their pain
directly and to accept an active role in the events of the period.

The funeral director returned to the young woman the next day. SHe
expressed a desire to see the baby, and he explained how that would be
possible for her at a later time at the funeral home if she wished it.
She wanted to attend the funeral and burial. The baby would be named.
She decided to ask the father herself for permission to put his name on
the death certificate. What is surprising here is that on first mention
of the possibility, her inclination was not to approach him and in fact
not even to tell him what had happened, given that he had wanted her to
have an abortion. Subsequently, he gave the permission. She had
reacted initially to the question about the minister with a firm, "Well,
there won't be any. I hate priests." In discussion it turned out she
had had a bad experience with a priest. The funeral director invited
her to consider whether she might welcome an encounter with a gentle
priest of his acquaintance. After a day's reflection, she expressed an
interest in such a priest; he was later contacted, and her experience
was a good one. A modest casket was selected sight unseen. She insisted on paying for the funeral herself, though her resources were limited.
Arrangements were made for reduced payment over time.

Before he left that second day, the funeral director explained how
he would wrap the baby in two receiving blankets and place it in the
casket. If she were to stay with her decision to come, she could bring
anyone with her she wanted. He would show her the room where the baby
was to be in a closed casket. It would be up to her to decide how she
wanted to experience it. If she changed her mind, that would be fine
too. When she was able, and on the day of the funeral, she came to the
funeral home alone an hour and a half before the service was to begin.
She was shown where the baby was and asked if she would prefer the
funeral director's going in with her or being alone with the baby. SHe
entered the room alone and closed the door behind her. Over an hour
later she emerged with a pained and reddened face. She had confronted
the reality of her loss. She had dealt with her emotion her own way.
Prior to the service, the funeral director reentered the room where the

baby was and opened the casket.   Attached to the now rearranged receiving blankets was a pin which said simply, "God loves you."

SECTION THREE

CREATIVITY IN BEREAVEMENT AND GRIEF WORK

SECTION THREE

CREATIVITY IN BEREAVEMENT AND GRIEF WORK

Grief is one of the most fundamental and least well understood aspects of human experience. For example, what are the differences in grieving engendered by different types of loss? What, if anything, is distinctive in grief following death as contrasted with other occasions for grief? What precisely is the relationship between grieving prior to a death and that which comes after the death? What is the long-term impact of bereavement on an individual or family? How ought we to understand even such oft-used terms as "bereavement", "mourning", or "grief work"? In matters such as these we have much to learn in order to improve the educational and counseling services that are offered to the public. Each of the five chapters in this Section offers its own specific contribution towards that important goal.

In Chapter 7, Jeanne M. Harper looks broadly at different kinds of grief and competing theories of grief reactions and responses. Practical examples are employed to illustrate the articulation of these conceptual frameworks and to develop an imaginative account of "grief loops" or highs and lows in an evolving process. Such loops correspond to the lived experience of progress and set back. These "pits" and "plateaus", as Harper calls them, incorporate the many variables and divergent elements that enter into a particular grieving process. Thus, they help individuals to understand and perhaps to be a bit more tolerant of their own strong feelings which can often be frightening when first encountered.

In the context of Harper's elucidation, the next two chapters consider more closely two specific kinds of loss and ensuing consequences. In his long-term study of college students and their adaptation to loss, Louis E. LaGrand has been struck by the variety of experiences cited as significant losses and by the relative prominence given both to death-related losses and to broken love relationships. Here it is the comparison between loss due to death and that associated with severed love relationships that comes in for detailed exploration: how are the two events perceived; what are they taken to mean; the importance of individuality; patterns of emotional and physical reaction; and coping mechanisms employed. In the end, we are reminded that loss can take many forms, that the main point is the issue of significance to the person involved, and that similarities and differences between different types of losses are well worth further study.

Among death-related losses, the death of a child and its impact on parents is surely one of the most profound. In Chapter 9, Margaret S. Miles and Eva K. Brown Crandall introduce the very poignant search for meaning consequent upon parental bereavement. The difficult point at issue is the question of positive or negative growth that might be generated by the tragedy of a child's death. Without minimizing the great price paid in the pain of such a loss, Miles and Crandall have had the imagination to begin an investigation of what can be made out of its aftermath. Their work, therefore, along with that of LaGrand, contributes to filling in some of the details of our overall understanding of loss and bereavement.

One particular feature of bereavement often experienced by survivors is that of paranormal phenomena. In a context in which the unusual is often and may easily be confused with the abnormal, many bereaved persons are at first reluctant to reveal or acknowledge such "hallucinations." In fact, as Bonnie Lindstrom points out in Chapter 10, these phenomena are not at all atypical of bereavement. Further, they can be of several different types and yet, whatever their status, they are usually comforting or reassuring to those who experience them. Clearly, there is still much to be learned about such experiences. Lindstrom makes no pretense to have exhausted the subject; her concern is only to open it up for further discussion and exploration.

Much of the above deals with relatively short-term reactions to loss, those occurring in the first year or so. Thus, it is good for us also to have here the work of Patricia A. Hyland on long-term impact of death in a family. The very lengthy time frames that might be involved in this latter sort of grief reaction make it difficult to study. But Hyland's clinical case examples demonstrate the importance of longitudinal consideration in different types of bereavement, especially where successful resolution of the loss has not been achieved. It is evident that effective counseling and a full picture of grief work need to take into account this revealing perspective on loss.

PLATEAUS OF ACCEPTANCE; PITS OF PAIN

Jeanne M. Harper

...a remarkable thing began to happen to me. I noticed that for short periods the hurt lessened. I reached "plateaus of acceptance" in the midst of my grieving process. These "plateaus" were the beginning of my healing process.

Unsigned Reflection Paper
Human Growth and Development Class
University of Wisconsin-Green Bay, 1981

What is grief? Webster says it is an emotional suffering caused by bereavement of death. Earl A. Grollman, in his book Concerning Death: A Practical Guide for the Living (1), explains it as the intense emotion that floods life when a person's inner security system is shattered by an acute loss, usually the death of someone important in his or her life. Grief has been defined as having psychological, physiological, and social components. When bereavement and mourning are over, grief continues. This inner pain--the anguish and emptiness--is what is meant by grief. After death/loss, life is never quite the same. William Worden, asked at a workshop in Chicago "How long does grief last?", replied, "How high is the sky?" As human beings, we inevitably experience pains of grief. There is no limit to grief: grief defies time.

Types of Grief

From my own experience, both in grief counseling and death education, I have found it useful to utilize Robert Fulton's (2) classification of grief. He defines three types: anticipatory, preparatory, and actualized or survivor's grief. Although ministers, funeral directors, social workers, and death educators may witness all three kinds, the greater percentage of cases deal with actualized or survivor's grief which occurs after a death or loss. By contrast, anticipatory grief describes the pain a family, friend, or community experience once they are aware that someone they care about may die. A third type, preparatory grief, is experienced by the person who has knowledge of his or her own coming death or loss.

Fulton's classification has been helpful in describing grief to clients and to workshop participants, as well as being helpful to me as

---

Special Dedication to Aunt Kathryn and her spirit of life and death.

Editor: Karen N. Atwood, English Department, University of Wisconsin-Marinette Center, Marinette, Wis. A doctoral candidate at Ohio State University. She has previously edited two papers for Jeanne M. Harper: "Applying Gestalt to the Grieving Individual" (1981) and "Helping Teenagers Confront Their Fears and Feelings about Death: A Workshop Approach" (1982), which were published by FORUM for Death Education and Counseling, Inc.

a counselor in better understanding their grief work. With clients/
participants, I share other people's creative responses to grief in
order that they can feel free to individualize their own response. In a
session, I present examples like the following of actualized or survivor's grief:

> Several years ago, a father of two children under eight lost
> his wife unexpectedly in her mid 30's. He wanted to know what
> the children could do to give the loss a positive meaning. I
> suggested they write a final letter to their mother, telling
> her whatever they needed to tell her. They put the letter and
> also a prized possession of theirs into the coffin. Later the
> father shared how the letter writing had helped the children
> work through some hard feelings, to say things that were "un-
> thinkable" or "unmentionable." The activities enabled them
> to begin their grief work and deal with the reality of their
> mother's death.

> An uncle of mine died of lung cancer in his late 50's. His
> children felt an intense need to do one last act of love for
> him. The son suggested that they dig their father's grave.
> The girls finally agreed. As they dug, they cried and laughed
> as they remembered their father and various events in their
> family life. This acting out of their feelings was an excellent
> tool for their grief work. The process of remembering and the
> physical act of digging the grave allowed them to actualize their
> grief.

> A woman, in her early 50's, in the hospital for testing, was not
> having bowel movements. Each time staff visited her, she would
> say, "My husband will be here today." He never came. Her medical
> tests turned up no physical reason for her bowel impaction; how-
> ever, there was an emotional explanation. One day a nurse found
> her crying; while she comforted her, the patient finally revealed
> that her husband had died about a month earlier. Since then she
> had internalized her unwillingness to let go of him. A few days
> after she "owned" her loss, she was "intestinally" back in work-
> ing order, and her grief work had begun.

These cases illustrate several ways survivors have responded to their
pain. In cases of sudden death, their grief may be at a high level.

Sometimes, however, a death or loss is anticipated, and grief will
occur at a lower intensity. Fulton believes that this anticipatory
grief is essentially healthful, for it allows healing to begin before
the loss is actualized. When family members are able to foresee a
death, they have time to work through their initial feelings and share
them with their fellow family members and the dying person. They have
time to adapt, time to slowly adjust to their loved one's leaving. Of
course, many people use this time to deny that death is imminent. They
choose to bury their feelings and sometimes isolate the patient, not
allowing him to talk about dying or his needs and feelings. Anticipatory grief, however, can be healing and positive, as the following
examples illustrate:

A young woman knew her husband (in his mid 30's) had cancer of
the liver. She chose to attend my classes on death awareness a
few months after his first surgery. She knew then that they had
about a year. In the classes she was able to share freely, to
become aware of her feelings, to come to understand grief and
the importance of sharing the limited special time remaining
with her spouse. As a result, her grief work was underway before he died. Together they chose the funeral songs and readings; discussed what she should do financially after his death;
what she should do about a new car, etc.

Last winter a friend of mine lost her father from terminal cancer.
She said that knowing he would die and having time to prepare for
the death were beneficial for the family. They chose the casket,
arranged the funeral service, took care of legal matters, including
changing ownership of the car and house, and were enabled to accept
that his death was going to occur. Later my friend observed how
hard it must be when death is sudden and there is no time to prepare legally or financially or to say "I'm sorry," or "I forgive
you," or "I love you." She was truly grateful for the few months
the family had to anticipate her father's death, even though some
days were extremely hard as they watched him slowly die.

Preparatory grief, Fulton's third category, refers to the dying
person's reaction as he or she "prepares" for his or her own death.
Hospital staff, hospice workers, parish ministers, as well as grief
counselors may be involved with individuals who are experiencing this
type of emotional pain. There are various ways of "preparing" for
death: completing unfinished business, writing to friends and rela--
tives, putting feelings into words, giving and receiving forgiveness,
readying wills and insurance policies, putting scrapbooks and albums in
order, sharing in family reunions and gathering of friends. Persons
preparing for death may go through the process of "life review" (3) in
which they seek to find meaning and purpose in their life and in their
death. They may begin this life review at retirement, when a major
phase of life is ending and another beginning, or when death is imminent.

Preparatory grief can be handled creatively, as these examples that
I use in my counseling and workshops show:

A dying woman in a local hospice program pulled her family of
origin together after many years of hard feelings. She was in
her mid 30's, with one child. She had breast cancer which later
metastasized. She was going to die, and she wanted something
good to come from it. She devoted her energy to rebuilding her
family support system. She called the family together, confronted them with their petty feuds, and encouraged them to
share time with each other. Later she observed that she was
ready to die since she had fulfilled a purpose: bringing her
family together.

A man in his early 70's was dying and very depressed. Since the
hospital staff did not have time to listen to all his life

Figure 1

GRIEF THEORIES*

*as applied to Bowlby's Grief Loop

Bowlby (survivor)

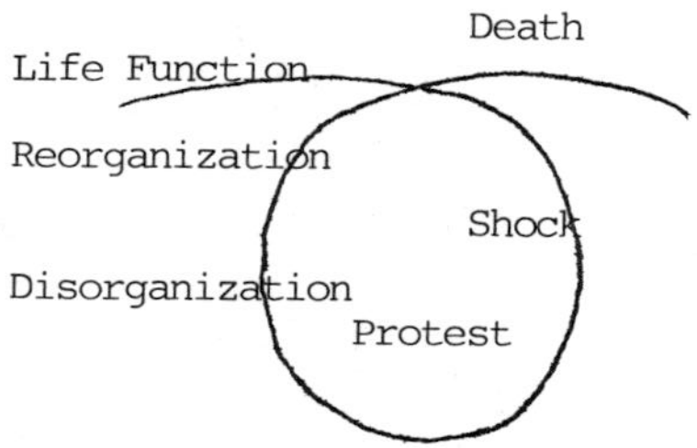

Death

Life Function

Reorganization

Disorganization

Shock

Protest

Grief and Growth Loop

Kubler-Ross (dying)

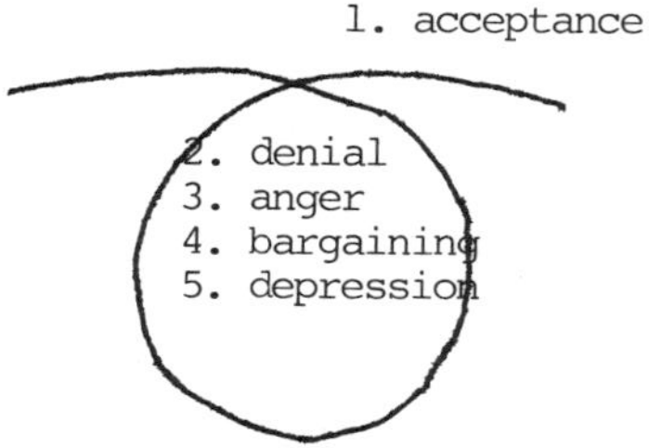

1. acceptance

2. denial
3. anger
4. bargaining
5. depression

Stages of Coping with Dying

Kavanaugh (survivor)

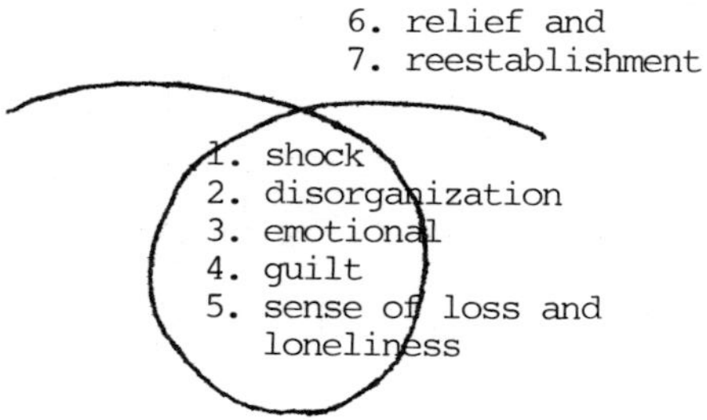

6. relief and
7. reestablishment

1. shock
2. disorganization
3. emotional
4. guilt
5. sense of loss and
   loneliness

Stages of Survivor

Havighurst (survivor)

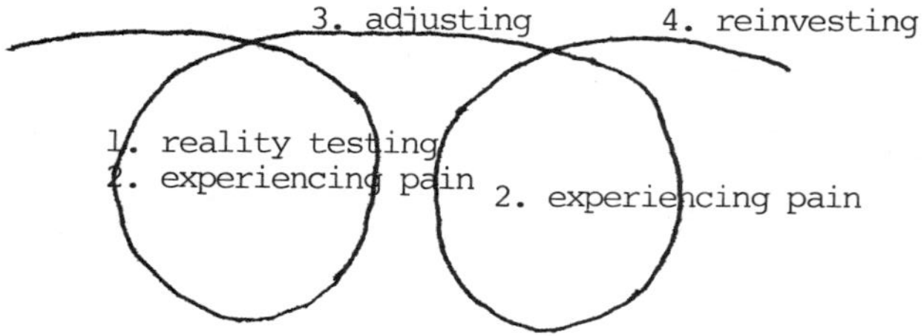

3. adjusting   4. reinvesting

1. reality testing
2. experiencing pain   2. experiencing pain

Tasks of Grief

94

stories, they found a way for him to "review" his life. He was given a recorder and tapes to share his life history. Through this process, his depression lifted; he found meaning for his life. After he died, the hospital staff sent the tapes to his daughter in California. She appreciated greatly receiving his unique gift of reminiscences.

My aunt, in her late 40's, developed cancer which metastasized throughout her body in a few months. She had been hospitalized a number of times and finally began to feel better. She asked to leave the hospital and go home for a family reunion. I shall never forget that day. Everyone in the family gathered around her bed out under the apple trees. She gave each of us special time with her alone. Then we sang every song she could remember. She invited us to look at the scrapbooks and picture albums she had out to help us remember our shared past—the good times, and the hard times. By her courage and her example, she taught us what it means to be fully alive—to fully live each day and to have few regrets when the final day comes.

In dealing with clients or workshop participants, I blend Fulton's ideas along with other recognized theories explaining grief reactions and responses, among them those of Kubler-Ross (4), Kavanaugh (5), Havighurst (6), and Bowlby (7). Very briefly, Kubler-Ross' stages of dying include denial, anger, bargaining, depression, and acceptance. Kavanaugh's stages of the survivor include shock, disorganization, emotional upset, guilt, sense of loss and loneliness, and finally relief and reestablishment. Havighurst's four tasks of grief include testing of reality, experiencing the pain, adjusting, and reinvesting. Bowlby's explanation of grief identifies shock/protest, disorganization, and ultimately reorganization.

Expansion of Grief Loop

Bowlby's "grief loop" can easily be expanded into a process. (See Figure 1) As a loss is actualized, the griever enters the loop. Since each person is unique, it stands to reason that his or her responses to loss will be unlike anyone else's. On the basis of my counseling experience, I believe that grief work continues after this initial loop Bowlby has identified, wherein emotions and feelings are very intense. I see grief as a continuing loop series of "pits" and "plateaus", points at which the grieved begins to adjust. (I have appropriated these terms, "pits" and "plateaus", from an unsigned reflection paper by a college student describing his reactions to grief. He pointed out that in the middle of the grieving process, there were breaks or plateaus— stages Bowlby does not include in his theory.) In the continuing loop, there will be lapses, plunges back into grief, sometimes triggered by very minor happenings. Earl Grollman speaks to his point in his book Living When A Loved One Has Died (8):

...and then suddenly just when you are making great strides forward you receive a startling setback. I may happen on a holiday, birthday, anniversary, or it may be triggered by your favorite song being played on the radio. You

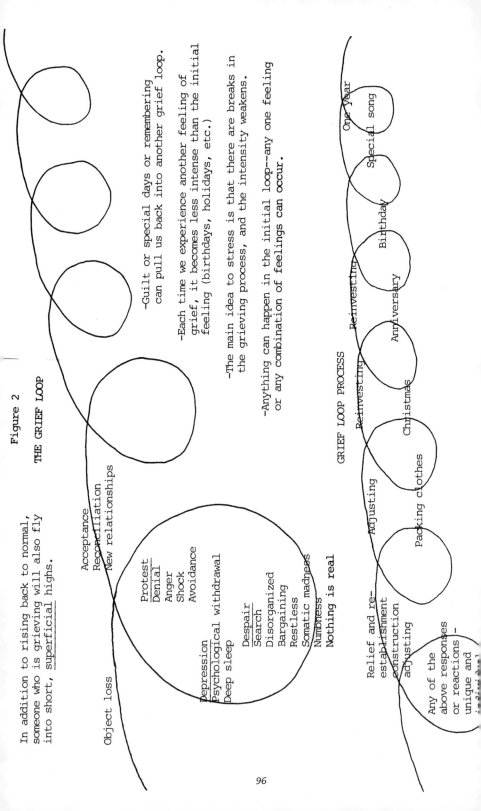

Figure 2

THE GRIEF LOOP

In addition to rising back to normal, someone who is grieving will also fly into short, superficial highs.

Object loss

Acceptance
Reconciliation
New relationships

Protest
Denial
Anger
Shock
Avoidance

Depression
Psychological withdrawal
Deep sleep

Despair
Search
Disorganized
Bargaining
Restless
Somatic madness
Numbness
Nothing is real

-Guilt or special days or remembering can pull us back into another grief loop.

-Each time we experience another feeling of grief, it becomes less intense than the initial feeling (birthdays, holidays, etc.)

-The main idea to stress is that there are breaks in the grieving process, and the intensity weakens.

-Anything can happen in the initial loop--any one feeling or any combination of feelings can occur.

GRIEF LOOP PROCESS

Relief and re-establishment
construction
adjusting

Any of the above responses or reactions - unique and individual

Packing clothes
Adjusting
Christmas
Reinvesting
Anniversary
Reinvesting
Birthday
Special song
One Year

think you are back to where it all started--at the bitter
moment of death. But remember, anguish, like ecstasy, is
not forever.

In the grieving process, as I understand it, there are a series of
loops connecting the griever's pits and plateaus; with each succeeding
loop, the pain weakens. (See Figure 2.) Gradually, the grieving person
begins to adjust and reinvest in new relationships and in life.   There
may be many loops before one feels that his or her feet are again firmly
on the ground, and each loop may present a new emotion. In reality, a
griever experiences many different feelings, and many different
responses are possible. The important point to recognize is that there
are breaks in the grieving, places where a feeling of acceptance may be
achieved--if only temporarily. Shneidman's observation (9) that a
griever goes back and forth between denial and acceptance supports my
view that the grief loop is indeed a process.

I have found the concept of loops or processes generally useful in
my work as a grief counselor and educator. In workshops, I direct the
participants to draw their "life loops" and then to label each loop. I
ask them to notice the space (time) between loops; the size and shape of
each loop; the number/frequency of upward/positive loops, as well as
downward/negative loops. Then I ask them to share the significance of
their life loop processes. (See Figure 3.) With grieving clients, I
ask them to draw their grief loops since the loss occurred. Later, in
therapy, they draw their lifeloops. I have seen remarkable progress in
grief work and in the "getting on with life" after clients discuss/
share/compare these two sets of drawings. Grievers see that there have
been other downward loops in their lives and realize that they have made
it through those pits of the past and reached plateaus of acceptance.
They believe that they can do so again.

Tasks of Grief

Havighurst's tasks of grief, discussed by Worden (6), integrate
well into my conceptual understanding of the grief loop process.
Reality testing and experiencing the pain (Tasks 1 and 2) fall within
the initial loop (See Figure 1). Between loops, the griever may go
through a number of ups and downs, adjusting to the changed environment
(Task 3). When the loops begin to reduce in intensity, the griever
reinvests time and energy in new relationships and experiences (Task 4).

Grief Variables

Variables or "determinants" (10) play a part in how someone handles
either a death or an anticipated death or loss. Professionals dealing
with the grieving person should take into account the following:

1. Relationship to deceased. Spouse, sibling, friend, grand-
    parent, etc.; age and sex of survivor and deceased.

2. Nature of the attachment. Strength of the attachment; amount
    of love that was involved; security involved; degree of depend-
    ence on the deceased for self-esteem; ambivalence--love/hate.

Figure 3

THE LIFE LOOP

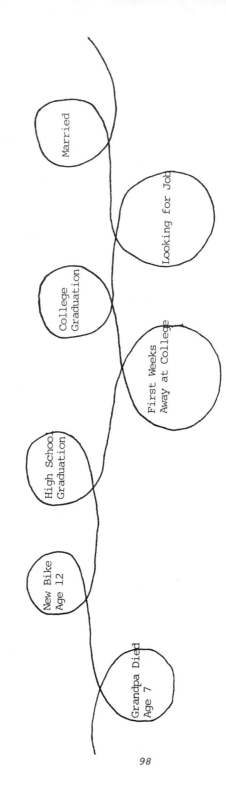

Each Life Loop is UNIQUE.

Shapes, spaces, sizes, etc. all vary! As do the number/frequency both of upward/positive loops and of downward/negative loops!

(If ambivalence is high, grief work can be very difficult since anger and guilt may be involved.)

3. <u>Mode of death</u>. Natural death, suicide, murder, accident, <u>length of illness</u>, place of death. There may be anger at the person who died, or anger at the person who caused a fatal accident. If the death occurs after a long illness, the survivor may have guilt for feeling relieved when it is over.

4. <u>History of other losses and coping skills</u>. Life change events, how past losses were dealt with (both personally and vicariously), little "daily" deaths.

5. <u>Personality variables</u>. Introversion (keeping feelings inside); extroversion (expressing them openly).

6. <u>Social variables</u>. Support system for the griever (ethnic, religious, cultural, subcultural).

Failures to Grieve

Many times there are variables that cause a breakdown in the grief process. William Worden shared a number of these causes at a conference in Chicago (6):

1. <u>Mobile society</u>. Deceased may die 2,000 miles away; neighbors may be unaware of the death or may not have known the person who died.

2. <u>Moral situations</u>. In some cases there may not be anyone to talk to about the loss or the whole subject may be socially/morally unacceptable; for example, suicide, loss of a baby through abortion, placing a baby up for adoption, loss of a gay lover, a secretive love affair.

3. <u>Personality traits</u>. Strong role person puts up a front-- hiding behind a reputation of handling everything.

4. <u>Inappropriate setting</u>. As in <u>Private Benjamin</u>, dying during intercourse, during a hair transplant. (11)

5. <u>Uncertain loss</u>. Soldier missing in action; apparent drowning; divorce, physical losses (body functions).

Grief Situations

Many feel the only cause for grief is death. As educators and counselors, it is very important we understand there are many situations which may cause an individual to grieve. Some of these are:

1. <u>Loss by divorce or separation</u>. The termination of a marriage

seems never to be final. The former spouse periodically
comes into the picture: to see the children, to go to court,
etc.

2. Loss of body functions. I myself have suffered various losses
   of body functions. Some days I find I can handle my losses
   quite easily; there are other days when I am in the "pits". I
   may be full of pain, and sometimes it's not just physical pain
   --it is emotional pain. Adapting to the loss of a body
   function, an extremity, or a sense seems to be similar.

3. Retirement. Plans for retirement may bring anticipated grief
   to the family/spouse and preparatory grief to the retiree.
   When retirement happens, he or she may feel actualized grief.

4. A child leaves home for college or marriage or employment.
   The parent(s), as well as the child, may go through a preparatory or anticipatory grief.

5. Death of a pet. Loss of a goldfish, bird, dog, cat, horse--
   whatever--usually constitutes a person's first grief loop.
   Later in life, other grief situations may reflect how one
   handled that initial loss. College students writing about
   their first experience with death have remembered building
   a coffin out of popsicle sticks for a goldfish/caterpillar;
   most remembered the burial technique: who did what, what
   they sang, what they read, where they buried the deceased.

6. Other grief situations might include loss of personal
   possessions (a wallet or purse), change of plans (cancellation
   of wedding), change of residence (moving, disaster), loss or
   change of employment, loss or change of significant personal
   relationships.

Grief Work

Grief work must be done. Grief work will be done. Sooner or
later, correctly or incorrectly, completely or incompletely,
in a creative or distorted manner, the work will be done. (12)

Grief can be expressed and responded to in both positive and
negative ways. Verbalization enhances awareness; the need to keep
telling others how the death occurred helps the griever to unload his
feelings. Emotional release should be encouraged, for it allows the
griever to actualize and accept the loss. Intellectual knowledge of the
loss becomes emotional knowledge. Grief needs to be expressed. If it
is not discharged, it may be explosive. Grief resembles steam in a
steam engine; unless it can escape in a controlled way, pressure builds
up and the boiler will explode (12).

Grief work must be done. Grief work will be done. In his study of
Coconut Grove, Lindemann (13) explains that grief work allows the
griever to be set free from "bondage to the deceased" in order to be

able to live an independent life with an "image of the deceased"; that is, one is able to live constructively with the memories, the hurts, the joys, and the sorrows. Lindemann believes that no griever ever escapes the process or breaks free until that person has worked through his or her grief. Therefore, a succession of loops and breaks, ups and downs, occurs for the bereaved, as grief work continues and with time, the initial pain diminishes. Samuel Johnson described this diminishing effect memorably, back in the eighteenth century in <u>Rasselas</u>:

> Distance has the same effect on the mind as on the eye, and while we glide along the stream of time, whatever we leave behind us is always lessening, and that which we approach increases in magnitude.

Expressions of Grief

The griever may express pain outwardly or inwardly; but in one way or another the feelings need to be expressed. To repress feeling is mentally and physically detrimental. Repressing emotions is a sign of <u>stress</u> not <u>strength</u> (14). In my workshops, I ask participants to brainstorm how they normally express their feelings of sad, mad, glad, excited. During the grieving process, they will draw on their established patterns verbal or nonverbal--inward or outward. Persons in grief may express their feelings in a variety of activities:

> writing, sleeping, withdrawing, meditating, running, jogging, painting, crying, screaming, pounding, twisting, talking, kneading bread dough (baking), scrubbing floors, cleaning drawers/closets/houses.

Patterns of Grief

As we look at the various ways individuals can handle their response and reactions to grief, we recognize certain patterns (6):

David Detached -- analytically observes the death; a very "cool" individual.

Stanley Sickly -- experiences intestinal or stomach problems, headaches, ulcerative colitis, rheumatoid arthritis, asthma, and cancer.

Willy Withdraw -- licks his wounds and withdraws from support groups/society; is an introvert.

Weeping Wilma -- cries, screams. An extrovert who expresses emotions physically and behaviorally.

Angie Anger -- verbalizes rage, fury. An extrovert who expresses emotions physically and emotionally.

Glenda Guilt -- feels remorse; "could have done more," "if only", "would have but", "should have".

As Worden points out, responses can appear at any stage in the grief process and they may change from loop to the next.

Conclusion

The grieving individual needs to know that his or her feelings are not bad or good; feelings simply are. He or she needs to name those feelings, acknowledge them, hold them, hug those feelings. Until one becomes aware of what he or she is doing or feeling and takes responsibility for those actions or feelings, one cannot change in any way.

Some people ask when grief is finished. "How high is the sky?" Maybe grief is passing when it turns from a physically and emotionally painful sadness to a sweet sadness. Or when the griever can think about the death without physical pain. Or when the person begins to reinvest energy in someone or something else. In her poem, "Lament," the poet, Edna St. Vincent Millay reminds us that daily life must continue:

> Anne, eat your breakfast;
> Dan take your medicine!
> Life must go on;
> I forget just why.

The grieving individual can do something to ease his or her pain. Such a person can seek out his or her own security and self-sufficiency. The best investment for an easier grief is to have the knowledge and the self-confidence that one can survive alone. The grieving person must find new projects to fulfill, new attachments to form, new dreams to live out. In Viktor Frankl's words (15):

> If we are truly faithful to the living spirit of the deceased, if we truly love them, we will continue our journey to perfection without the chains of self pity and pessimism.

That is the challenge to the grieving person as he or she moves through ups and downs, from pits of pain to plateaus of acceptance.

References

1. Grollman, E.A. Concerning Death: A Practical Guide for the Living. Boston: Beacon Press, 1974.

2. Fulton, R. A Psychological Aspect of Terminal Care: Anticipatory Grief. Symposium at Columbia University, November 6, 1970.

3. Butler, R.N. The Life Review: An Intepretation of Reminiscence in the Aged. In L.R. Allman and D.R. Jaffee (eds.) Readings in Adult Psychology. New York: Harper and Row, 1978.

4. Kubler-Ross, E. On Death and Dying. New York: Macmillan, 1969.

5. Kavanaugh, R.E. Facing death. Baltimore: Penguin Books, 1974.

6. Worden, W. Grief Therapy and Grief Counseling. University of Chicago Workshop, March 1980. Presentation included Havighurst's "Tasks of Grief."

7. Bowlby, J. Separation Anxiety. International Journal of Psycho-analysis, 1960, 41, 89-113.

8. Grollman, E.A. Living When a Loved One Has Died. Boston: Beacon Press, 1977.

9. Shneidman, E.S. Deaths of Man. Baltimore: Penguin, 1974.

10. Weisman, A.D. Is Mourning Necessary. In B. Schoenberg (ed.), Anticipatory Grief. New York: Columbia University Press, 1974.

11. Zinner, E. FORUM Foundation Workshop, July 1982.

12. Robbins, H.W. Grief. Grand Rapids, MI: Zondervan, 1976.

13. Lindemann, E. Symptomatology and Management of Acute Grief. American Journal of Psychiatry, 1944, 101, 141-148.

14. Johnson, W. Coursework through Winona State University for Wisconsin State Social Workers Association at Green Bay, 1979.

15. Frankl, V. Man's Search for Meaning. Boston: Pocket Books, 1974.

THE BREAKUP OF A LOVE RELATIONSHIP

AS A "DEATH REACTION"

Louis E. LaGrand

During the past four years the author conducted a study of the losses and loss reactions of college students. It began in an attempt to grasp the plight of students who were confronted with the death of a loved one and had to work through the greater part of the grief process away from home and family. In collecting data for the project the key question students were asked was: "What is your most recent major loss?" The respondents were then asked to indicate the physical and emotional reactions accompanying this loss, how they coped with their reactions and whether or not they could have been better prepared to deal with the entire situation.

The research involved 2,502 students from a variety of academic and cultural backgrounds at fourteen institutions of higher education in New York State and Vermont. One of the early surprises in the study was the large number (over 50) of different losses which students perceived as "major" losses in their lives and from which a grief response ensued. Of prime concern for this paper was the analysis of emotional and physical reactions, as well as coping responses, to losses involving death of a loved one and the breakup of a love relationship. It should be noted that nearly 75% of all losses reported involved the separation from a significant other through death, divorce, temporary geographical separation, a dissolved friendship, or the breakup of a love relationship. By far the two most frequent separations reported were due to deaths or broken love relationships. Therapists believe that the grief response associated with divorce is as devastating as the response to death (1,2,3). Although there are many divorces each year, there are many more breakups of intimate male-female relationships than most people realize (4). The data reported herewith suggest that a break up produces symptoms which are as intense and long lasting in students as those which surface when death occurs.

The Perception of Loss

Before we examine data to support the contention that the breakup of a love relationship can be as traumatic as the death of a loved one, it is important to analyze the role of perceptions and beliefs as they affect loss reactions. Perceptions are the personal meanings we give to experiences. They vary immensely among individuals. Two people can look at an event and perceive it differently--they draw different meaning from it. Perceptions are based on a number of variables including opportunities to perceive, age, self-concept, the experience of threat, and the nature of the physical organism (5). The literature on the grief process is replete with phrases and descriptions like those found in an education textbook for beginning teachers. Emphasis is placed on words such as "individuality", "uniqueness", "very personal", or "one's own grief." These descriptions draw attention to differences in grief styles as we would draw attention to the vast differences in lifestyles. Furthermore, we need only examine the differences in dying styles and the recognition that all do not die according to a specific model. In a more critical vein, there is much controversy over whether each dying person should be told of their condition at the time of discovery. To tell everyone, it is argued, leaves no room for individuality and the fact that some may not want to be told, even if they suspect it (6).

The importance of understanding individuality in the grief process must not be underestimated. It affects our own response to loss as well as our approach to assisting others in a counseling or therapeutic relationship. A close examination of individual differences will help in our analysis of the breakup of a love relationship as a "death reaction."

Beginning with anatomical differences we need only recall that no two people have the same finger or voice prints. When you consider the millions of people in the United States alone, this is truly an amazing distinction. Examine the variations in taste for foods; some people like salty food, others abhor it. Fish is a delicacy for some, poison for others. Tastes in clothes are sharply diverse depending on custom, culture, and family influence. The same temperature affects people in rather contrasting ways. The effects, particularly side effects, of drugs may cause one person to break out in a rash and another to become nauseated even though each consumes identical doses. Pain thresholds are uniquely individual ranging from super sensitive to mildly painful given the same external stimulus. Learning styles vary; some people are visual learners, others auditory, still others tactile learners, and some are combinations of these three modalities.

Few researchers have studied the critical implications of biochemical and emotional individuality more than Roger Williams, the internationally known biochemist. In his classic, You Are Extraordinary (7), he writes:

> We may be sent to the same schools, we may wear similar clothes, speak similarly and follow many of the same customs, live in similar houses, have the same amusements offered us, and have access to the same newspapers and books. But because the same messages do not come to us from the outside world, and because the interpretive apparatus of each of us is distinctive, we do not turn out to be uniform.

It is important to focus on the fact that we do not possess the same interpretive apparatus and that the messages from the outside world differ within each of us. These messages differ substantially with the meaning of loss.

What are the implications of individuality applicable to understanding loss and the resulting grief response? Here is a sample of possibilities:

1) Adaptation takes place on different levels. The same loss will call forth entirely different responses from

principal grievers. Every student does not adapt (accept the new environment without the "object" of loss) in the same way. Nor should we expect them to conform to <u>our</u> norms of adaptation.

2) Immediate reactions to loss range from feelings of shock and numbness, to anger at various people, to deep guilt, or to an unusual lack of response, even denial that the event took place.

3) It does not necessarily follow that the closer the griever is related to the deceased, the stronger the grief reaction. Grief may be more demanding when a grandmother dies than when a parent dies or for a roommate than a brother.

4) Finally, the same type of loss also impacts in the long term quite differently on students. Their changes in behavior are powerful metaphors reflecting negative or positive consequences of loss experiences.

The lesson to be learned involves the realization that although there are similarities in responses to major loss there are also behaviors which we cannot foresee, do not expect, understand, or agree with.

At the core of individuality and perception of loss are one's beliefs. What we believe to be true about ourselves and our environment is the basis for behavior (8,9). For instance, the power of belief about what a drug will do is astonishing. It influences the development of addiction or dependency and even how a substance will react when ingested as so many placebo experiments have demonstrated. Historically, there is much evidence linking the cause of disease with attitudes. Recently, dramatic changes in the impact of cancer on individuals has been demonstrated (10). Beliefs about the social value of individuals in caring relationships influence how a helping professional cares for those individuals (11).

What kinds of beliefs about loss are held by students and influence behavior? Here are some typical responses:

1. "Loss is what happens to others, not me."
2. "Loss is punishment for something I have done wrong."
3. "Loss can be avoided and I am unlucky when it does occur."
4. "Losses such as death are unnatural."
5. "I refuse to believe our relationship will ever end."

What one expects to happen when loss occurs, if these beliefs are held, will have a major impact on how he or she copes with the loss. Such beliefs are the basis for negative expectations when loss occurs. We tend to see what we expect to see based on past experiences or what significant others suggest will happen (12). The tragic aftermath of negative beliefs is part of the reason for reactions of neurotic guilt, excessive anger, constant denial, withdrawal from all relationships, and physical sickness. Just as our thought processes affect the course of a disease, as well as its treatment, so too can they become the deciding factor in how we choose to grieve a loss.

Comparing Loss Reactions

With the awareness of the influence of perceptions and beliefs on loss behavior let us examine the specific reactions of students to the losses of death and the breakup of a love relationship. Of 1,322 students reporting these losses, 696 said the death of a loved one was their most recent major loss and 626 said the breakup of a love relationship was their most recent major loss. Deaths of loved ones included grandparents, parents, or friends and the quality of relationship with the deceased was a pivotal factor in the grief response. The corrected chi square statistic was used in comparing student responses.

The data were obtained from students (802 women and 520 men) representing a relatively stable, small urban and rural, predominantly white population. The average student age was 20 with 19.3 percent of the sample being freshmen, 25.6% sophomores, 27.5% juniors, 28.6% seniors, and with 84.1% from hometowns with less than 100,000 population. A survey instrument, designed and pretested on 115 university students, consisted of five check-off and two open-ended questions, and was experimenter administered. Exclusive of demographic data, 16,717 observations were collected on grief reactions. The two open-ended questions resulted in an additional 1,800 written responses.

Feelings

Beginning with a comparison of feelings associated with these losses, notice (Table 1) that a wider variety of feelings is reported when a breakup of a love relationship occurs. More students experienced shock, disbelief, fear, and helplessness with death than with the loss of a love relationship. A closer examination of the many feelings involved in the latter gives indication of the strong impact and variation of responses that breakup causes in the lives of students. Anger, guilt, loneliness, hatred, rejection, and depression were more frequently reported and carry powerful and emotional connotations. In addition, frustration, self-pity, emptiness, reduction in self-confidence, and a feeling of being lost were all more frequently experienced with the severed love relationship. As in most studies of grief, depression was the single most frequently reported feeling (82.1% for a breakup, 69.8% for death). There was no significant difference in students' denial associated with either of the losses.

What causes very strong emotional reactions, prolonging the intensity and length of the grief process, are feelings of rejection. Over half of the students reporting the breakup of a love relationship said they felt rejection, while only fifteen students (2.2%) indicated this feeling when death occurred.

The specific impact of a breakup is graphically illustrated by the following statement made one year after a loss occurred:

Table 1

FEELINGS ACCOMPANYING LOSS AND CORRECTED CHI SQUARE VALUES

	DEATH	LOVE RELATIONSHIP	CORRECTED CHI SQUARE
	[1] (N = 696)	(N = 626)	
1. Shock	435 (62.5%)	185 (29.6%)	142.33*
2. Disbelief	365 (52.4%)	194 (31.0%)	61.27*
3. Helplessness	299 (43.0%)	193 (30.8%)	20.23*
4. Fear	193 (27.7%)	122 (19.5%)	11.88*
	LOVE RELATIONSHIP	DEATH	
	(N = 626)	(N = 696)	
1. Depression	514 (82.1%)	486 (69.8%)	26.31*
2. Loneliness	490 (78.3%)	232 (33.3%)	266.73*
3. Emptiness	456 (72.8%)	382 (54.9%)	45.02*
4. Anger	370 (59.1%)	288 (41.4%)	40.71*
5. Frustration	338 (54.0%)	204 (29.3%)	81.99*
6. Rejection	320 (51.1%)	15 (2.2%)	415.04*
7. Self-Confidence	291 (46.5%)	25 (3.6%)	331.00*
8. Guilt	199 (31.8%)	180 (25.9%)	5.37*
9. Self-Pity	194 (31.0%)	78 (11.2%)	77.72*
10. Hatred	153 (24.4%)	46 (6.6%)	80.56*
11. Lost	149 (23.8%)	108 (15.5%)	13.91*

[1] Note the greater number of students in this sample.
* P less than .01
** P less than .05

Table 2

PHYSICAL REACTIONS ACCOMPANYING LOSS AND CORRECTED CHI SQUARE VALUES

PHYSICAL REACTION	DEATH	LOVE RELATIONSHIP	CORRECTED CHI SQUARE
	[1](N = 696)	(N = 626)	
Crying	543 (78.0%)	438 (70.0%)	10.73*
Numbness	87 (12.5%)	45 (7.2%)	9.76*
Chills	82 (11.8%)	22 (3.5%)	29.94*
	LOVE RELATIONSHIP	DEATH	
	(N = 626)	(N = 696)	
Insomnia	280 (44.7%)	230 (33.0%)	18.49*
Digestive Disturbances	158 (25.2%)	109 (15.7%)	18.17*
Vomiting	28 (4.5%)	13 (1.9%)	6.60*

[1] Note the greater number of students in this sample.
* P less than .01

I started feeling like my world was falling down around me
and everything was going wrong. While talking to my sister,
I remember telling her that I wanted to quit school, go
home, and just end everything. For me, losing my loved one
(to another girl), whom I had known since my second week at
college, was like losing a big part of myself. I suddenly
felt like I couldn't face life.

Physical Reactions

The physical reactions accompanying these major losses were quite
similar. Headaches, exhaustion and weakness, backaches, nausea, skin
rash, labored breathing, and feeling cold were not significantly
different in terms of number of students reporting these reactions.
More students indicated that crying, numbness, and chills were
associated with death while insomnia, digestive disturbances, and
vomiting more frequently accompanied the breakup of a love relationship
(Table 2). Insomnia is a common reaction in many loss experiences.
Twice as many students reported vomiting when a breakup occured
suggesting a stronger reaction to the severed love relationship (4.5% to
1.9%). A greater number also reported digestive disturbances (25.2% to
15.7%). Many students indicated a great loss of appetite accompanied
their depression as the following statements illustrate.

1) ...I was totally devastated. For the first five days,
I did not eat anything substantial. I only could manage
to drink down orange juice. I moped around like a lost
puppy...

2) My level of concentration was low and it became difficult
to study for any length of time. My appetite had become very
irregular and my stomach felt as though it had been clenched
into a tight ball.

A description of physical reactions involved in the breakup of a
love relationship often parallels or is identical to the classic
symptoms found in the literature on death reactions (13). The young
woman in the following response indicates the intensity of her physical
reactions.

For two weeks I was miserable--I had a constant headache it
seemed, and I just couldn't sleep very well at night. I'd
get up in the morning and feel tired before I even started
my day. I cried a lot during those two weeks. All in all,
I could consider myself a wreck during that time. I even
began doubting myself as unworthy of having a relationship
with anyone at this stage. In a sense I considered myself
a failure for what happened.

A male student willing to discuss or write about his physical reactions
to a breakup was often very difficult to find. Males tended to minimize
their feelings and seemed less willing to share them and be open about
what had happened. However, one such student wrote the following in
describing his physical response to his major loss of a girlfriend:

Table 3

COPING MECHANISMS AND CORRECTED CHI SQUARE VALUES

COPING MECHANISM	DEATH	LOVE RELATIONSHIP	CORRECTED CHI SQUARE
	[1](N = 696)	(N = 626)	
1. Crying	492 (70.7%)	410 (65.5%)	3.86**
2. Family Support	374 (53.7%)	155 (24.8%)	114.07*
3. Thinking of All the Good Things	332 (47.7%)	189 (30.2%)	41.58*
4. Religious Beliefs	243 (34.9%)	84 (13.4%)	80.64*
	LOVE RELATIONSHIP	DEATH	
	(N = 626)	(N = 696)	
1. Talking About It	503 (80.4%)	478 (68.7%)	22.85*
2. Support of Friends	418 (66.8%)	348 (50.0%)	37.36*
3. Time	405 (64.7%)	370 (53.2%)	17.60*
4. Developing New Relationships	339 (54.2%)	29 (4.2%)	407.46*
5. Keeping Busy	330 (52.7%)	224 (32.3%)	56.22*
6. Writing My Feelings	194 (31.0%)	85 (12.2%)	68.67*
7. Replacement	166 (26.5%)	12 (1.7%)	171.75*
8. Developing New Interests	153 (24.4%)	20 (2.9%)	132.89*
9. Learning to Relax My Body	49 (7.8%)	27 (3.9%)	8.76*

[1] Note the greater number of students in this sample.
* P less than .01
** P less than .05

The physical feelings I got were intense at the time. I had no energy and felt sluggish. I just wanted to stay in bed all day. My stomach tended to be on the queasy side consistently. I had a very small appetite, my excretion system was all messed up, and I appeared absent-minded to others around me.

There were no significant differences in the following physical reactions associated with both losses: headaches, nausea, weakness, exhaustion, backaches, cold skin rashes, and labored breathing.

Coping Mechanisms

More students use a greater variety of coping mechanisms in dealing with the loss of a love relationship than in dealing with the death of a loved one (Table 3). Family support, memories, religious beliefs, and crying were more frequently listed as coping mechanisms when confronting the death of a loved one. Twice as many coping responses were listed by students when dealing with a breakup of a love relationship (9 to 4). Support of roommates and friends was much more prevalent in dealing with a breakup. Those students who turn to family for support usually involve the mother as the chief support person. Each of the following coping mechanisms were more frequently used by students dealing with the breakup of a love relationship than by students dealing with the death of a loved one: talking about it, replacement, keeping busy, developing new interests, developing new relationships, learning to relax, time, and writing about one's feelings. Samples of the written responses of students describing how they coped with their breakups suggest much variation in coping techniques. The first one that follows indicates the typical support of roommates during the crisis and how important they are as support persons. The second seeks a psychologist to help her, while the third, in conjunction with a roommate, utilizes ridicule and sarcasm to cope.

1) My roommate was my target. She was willing to talk to me luckily. I guess I expected her to save the day. I did get my hopes up too high. She isn't God. Everything didn't all of a sudden change because I talked to her. She did help me a great deal though. First of all she got it into my head that the world wasn't going to end. She made it clear that I had to adjust and keep going. It made me feel better when she explained to me that she went through an experience like this, and that my feelings were not abnormal. My roommate suggested the various options that were open to me.

2) I went to see Dr. ___ the following day and totally broke down in his office. I kept blaming myself over and over again. He listened to what I had to say, then started to talk to me about my feelings. I had put so much guilt upon myself for the breakup of the relationship that I was causing me to lose touch with everything around me. My self-concept and ego were on the downward plummet when I decided to talk to Dr. ___. He told me ways to release my anger.

3) Since my roommate had been with us through the whole mess, she understood everything. She really was great because she understood why I resented his ego, his games, and his face! It may not be right, but snide remarks help let off steam. she joined in with me in the verbal abuse department. That's mostly how I coped--cutting him down to make myself feel better. I really haven't progressed much since then. Sarcasm is my biggest aid now. It still hurts me a lot to think how we were. I know he really did deceive me with his "open" character. I act the way I do now as a defense. Gary has hurt me immensely twice. I don't want to go for three.

In comparing student responses to loss it must be noted that the lack of systematic observation of students experiencing these losses limits the insights we can draw from the analysis of data. Also, the statistical responses do not contain a measure of intensity of reaction to the specific loss--which further hinders interpretation. There were no significant differences in the use of philosophical beliefs, acceptance, or drawing as coping mechanisms.

To sum up, the evidence suggests, but does not prove, there is equality of the grief response for some students to these two types of losses. A more decisive step must be pursued, namely, the analysis of responses of individual students who have experienced both the breakup of a love relationship and the death of a loved one. Nevertheless, it does not minimize the possibility that the nature and quality of a love relationship, coupled with the interpersonal sensitivity of a given student, is such that the breakup is perceived as a total rejection and the resulting grief response is truly a "death reaction." The following passage illustrates this point:

When I broke up with my boyfriend, I stayed in bed for two weeks without eating or moving--I just cried. My two best friends stayed with me the whole time, talking to me, telling me that I wasn't the only one who had to live through this, and that helped a lot because one my friends had already been through a major breakup, and it was comforting to keep hearing that she went through the same thing, and that I'd live. I really was in terrible shape, and I don't think I would have made it without them.

The tone of this response suggests intensity of reactions and emotional upheaval above that experienced in many grief responses associated with the death of a loved one.

Coping with Both Losses

Interviews with students who have experienced both losses, as well as anecdotal evidence submitted by students who have experience both losses, adds substantial weight to the hypothesis that some students perceive the loss of a love relationship in such a way as to consider their loss "worse than the death of a loved one." The nature of the relationship and love involved seems to be unique with each object of loss. That is, the nature of the bond between a student and a parent and the same student and a boyfriend is not the same.

A young woman whose father died when she was 14 years old and whose breakup with her fiance came six years later, said that she loved them both very deeply but that the type of love was somehow not the same. She remarked that the breakup affected her more. It was worse than anything she had been through. During an interview she blurted out, "I mean five years of me is gone." The type of personal investment in another person, whether father, mother, grandparent, fiance, or boyfriend appears to vary with the individual student. It does not imply that there is a greater love for one than the other. But somehow the characteristics of the relationships are very individual and affect the grief response in ways that are unknown. As an example, one and one-half years after a breakup, a young woman wrote the following: "I tried to date other people and tried to forget all of my feelings for that special person. I found that even after a year and a half all of those feelings are still there. I never had trouble getting dates, but no one ever made me feel as strong as he did." Once again, we see a belief pattern heavily influencing feelings and behavior. As indicated, if only that one person is capable of making her feel strong, she cannot be fully open to new relationships or to give up the old. Studies with more stringent methodology and controls are needed to uncover these subtle differences.

One rationale that students use in explaining why they feel that the breakup of a love relationship is so difficult an experience is the fact that "the person isn't really gone." That is, it is argued, that knowing the person is still around, seeing him or her again, opens old wounds and adds to their grief. This is especially true if they are seen with a new friend of the opposite sex. This is the tone of a response given by a male student who clearly believed that his breakup was worse than death.

> I have had many family members and friends die over the last few years and I feel that type of loss is much easier to handle. When my grandfather died, I saw him laid out and then buried and I knew he was gone. I then knew I had to go on with life. With Linda, I still see her almost every day and just seeing her keeps me from realizing it's over.

The Dependence/Independence Factor

It appears that a major variable involved in the intensity of the grief response to a severed love relationship is the degree of dependency that one had on the other during the relationship. There are many students who indicated that their dependency was the influencing factor in how difficult it was to work through the loss.

The result of dependency may take the form of great feelings of guilt for the loss. A number of students seemed to feel that "it was all my fault." Women especially appeared to blame themselves. Sometimes friends of one of the partners in the breakup complicated matters by implying that it was the other person's fault. Unfortunately, this led to a belief by the condemned that "I'm a bad person." Overdependency on another also limited one's relationships with peers and reduced the number of support persons who might normally be available during times of loss.

What did students say about being too dependent? Here are samples of their responses:

1) I think that I committed too much of myself in this relationship and in doing this I lost much of my self-identity. Thus, when the relationship ended, I was lost and disoriented. When I do meet someone again and I fall in love I'm going to make sure that me and the other person do not lose our own self-identity. I think it is possible to have a loving relationship and still maintain your self-identity.

2) If possible, try not to become so dependent on one person, whether it is your friend, lover, husband, wife, etc. Try to keep all your old friends and a variety of friends so if something should happen you'll be prepared and have others that you are close to help you accept and forget your loss.

3) An individual should not come to depend or rely on another individual to the extent that the other individual controls the life of the person in question.

These and many other responses point to the questions, "What is love?" and "What does a loving relationship consist of?" Once again it appears that how one perceives a relationship says much about how one grieves when that relationship ends. Also, how one views the self as a person (capable, good, flexible) plays a key role or as one student put it:

I went through a total identity crisis when he called things off. I was lost. I feel if I knew myself better and what I want for me, I wouldn't have been so hurt for so long. I probably would still feel hurt, but I would have been able to pick myself up easier. The only sure thing you have is yourself.

Conclusion and Implications

Having examined three data sources (frequency comparisons, written responses from those suffering the breakup of a love relationship, and those suffering both the death of a loved one and a breakup), we can observe the numerous physical and emotional reactions and coping mechanisms employed when a major loss occurs. It is apparent that a wide variety of coping mechanisms and feelings evolve when the breakup of a love relationship is confronted by some students. This research only identifies the type and frequency of reaction not the rationale for it.

There are numerous factors which affect the outcome of bereavement
(14). The personal meaning that a student gives to a loss event is the
pivotal factor in how the loss is assimilated into one's life. Every
student perceives through a different lens, through a different filter.

If the loss is viewed as catastrophic, despite what society or any
other person implies it to be, the individual grief response normally
follows a course which parallels the perceptions and beliefs of the
griever. Counselors, parents, and therapists need to be constantly
aware of the beliefs that the adolescent poses about loss as a developmental experience if they are to fully understand behavior which follows
the breakup of a love relationship. Such a loss seems to be a common
phenomenon in the lives of the young and an integral part of the
intimacy-distantiation factor of personality development as suggested by
Erikson(15). How they are assisted in their grief work can have a
lasting impact on how they cope with subsequent losses. Minimizing the
importance of this type of loss reduces the griever's willingness to
trust during times of crisis, thereby limiting social support.

By their written statements, students characterize their personal
reactions as intense and traumatic when a breakup occurs. Those who
have experienced both losses also indicate the acute emotional and
physical upheaval which accompanied their breakups. The tendency on the
part of some to believe that only death is a highly significant loss in
the lives of students should be questioned. Under some circumstances,
students grieve the breakup of a love relationship in ways which are
characteristic of a "death reaction" and some students perceive it as an
experience worse that the death of a loved one.

References

1. Hafer, W. Coping with Bereavement from Death or Divorce. Englewood Cliffs, N.J.: Prentice-Hall, Inc., 1981.

2. Smokes, S. Divorce. Syracuse Herald American, June 15, 1980.

3. Tanner, I. The Gift of Grief. New York: Hawthorn Books, 1976.

4. Hill, C., Rubin, Z. & Peplau, L. Breakups Before Marriage: The End of 103 Affairs. Journal of Social Issues, 1976, 32, 147-168.

5. Combs, A. & A.S.C.D. 1962 Yearbook Committee, Perceiving, Behaving, Becoming. Washington: A.S.C.D., 1962.

6. Barcley, V. Families Facing Cancer. Cancer News, Spring/Summer, 1970.

7. Williams, R. You are Extraordinary. New York: Pyramid Books, 1971.

8. Maltz, M. Psychocybernetics. New York: Pocket Books, 1969.

9. Hunter, E. Brainwashing: The Story of Men Who Defied It. New York: Pyramid Books, 1958.

10. Simonton, O., Simonton, S., & Creighton, J. Getting Well Again. New York: Bantam Books, 1980.

11. Combs, A., Avila, D., & Purkey, W. Helping Relationships: Basic Concepts for the Helping Professions. Boston: Allyn and Bacon, 1971.

12. Harman, W. Science and the Clarification of Values: Implications of Recent Findings in Psychological and Psychic Research. Journal of Humanistic Psychology, 1981, 21, (3), 3-15.

13. Lindemann, E. Symptomatology and Management of Acute Grief. American Journal of Psychiatry, 1944, 101, 141-148.

14. Parkes, C. Bereavement: Studies of Grief in Adult Life. New York: International Universities Press, 1972.

15. Erikson, E. Growth and Crisis of the Healthy Personality. In Kluckhohn, C., Murray, H., & Schneider, D. (eds.). Personality in Nature, Society, and Culture. New York: Alfred A. Knopf, 1953.

THE SEARCH FOR MEANING AND ITS POTENTIAL

FOR AFFECTING GROWTH IN BEREAVED PARENTS

Margaret Shandor Miles

Eva K. Brown Crandall

The loss of a loved one through death is virtually a universal human experience. Few individuals who live a normal life span can escape the experience of losing a close relative or friend. The grief process which characteristically follows such loss is considered one of life's most profound and unique human experiences (1).

In the past two decades, this process of grief has been examined, studied, and conceptualized by numerous authors from a wide variety of disciplines. The major focus of many of these publications has been on describing the cognitive, behavioral, emotional, and physical manifest-ations of grief (2-6) and on the evaluation of the outcomes of the grief experience on bereaved individuals (7-11). For the most part, the grief outcome studies have examined problematic, negative outcomes in an attempt to isolate variables that may be predictive of negative sequelae of grief, such as severe emotional problems, ill health, or early death. Less attention has been paid to the study of potentially positive outcomes that may occur in the bereaved. A number of authors, however, have mentioned the idea that grief, although very painful and difficult to endure, can potentially lead the sufferer to grow and mature as a human being (1, 6, 12-17). Koestenbaum, in particular, has noted:

> You do not know what it means to be human, you do not
> know the essence of your humanity, unless you have
> opened the window to your nature. And this window
> is opened only by suffering: pain, death and all the
> negative experiences of life. This is an ancient
> truth...Suffering leads to insight, to knowledge
> about what it really means to be. (14, p. 54)

Because of the unique relationship between parent and child, the death of a child has been identified as one of the most profound human losses. Children represent to parents a part of their own being and their immortality. In addition, the parental role carries with it a deep feeling of responsibility for the physical and emotional well-being of the child. The death of a child, then, sends the bereaved parents into a deep and painful existential "search for meaning." (18-20) This search has been articulated clearly by Frances Gunther in the epilogue to the book Death Be Not Proud:

> Death always brings one suddenly face to face with life.
> Nothing, not even the birth of one's child, brings one so

Reprinted from Health Values: Achieving High Level Wellness, 1983, 7, 19-23, by permission of the publisher, Charles B. Slack Inc.

close to life as his death...The impending death of one's
child raises many questions in one's mind and heart and
soul. It raises all the infinite questions, each answer
ending in another question. What is the meaning of life?
What are the relations between things: life and death?
the individual and the family? the family and society?
marriage and divorce? the politics and religion? man,
men, and God? (21, p. 250)

   In the conceptual model depicting the process of parental grief,
developed by one of the authors (Miles) (19-20), this "Search for
Meaning" has been identified as an extremely important aspect of the
grief process. Ultimately it may be a key factor in a positive "growth"
versus a negative "despair" resolution of the grief experience. To
learn more about this search for meaning and the subsequent impact on
one's views about life, open-ended data from bereaved parents collected
in three separate studies were examined in order to assess both the
positive "growth" resolutions and negative "despair" resolutions following the profound experience of losing a child through death. Specifically, the data were examined to determine how the death of a child
affected the parents' views about themselves, about others, and about
life in general.

Related Literature

   Hill, a family systems theorist, in his theoretical treatise about
factors affecting families under stress, points out the great importance
of the interpretation made by the family about a crisis event. This
interpretation which he defines as "meaning" is based on the family's
value system and its previous experiences with crisis. In his view,
families with adequate resources may still fail to deal adequately with
a crisis because they interpret it negatively rather than positively
(22-23).

   Coming from an existential theoretical base, Koestenbaum notes that
all individuals must make a fundamental decision regarding the overall
view they impose on life. Two choices are apparent: a
joyful/optimistic or a despairing/pessimistic view of life. According
to Koestenbaum, confronting death, grief, and suffering particularly in
one's own life, can contribute to a meaning of life that is optimistic
(14). One of the greatest contributors to the existential concept of
meaning is Victor Frankl, founder of the movement called Logotherapy.
In his theoretical framework, emphasis is placed on how an experience of
great pain can help us find our deepest meaning and conquer negative
attitudes. On the other hand, despair is caused by suffering in which
the sufferer sees no meaning. Frankl is not suggesting that one settle
back and adjust to a painful loss, but that one get in touch with the
feelings of outrage and anger and direct them into finding the meaning
of one's own existence (13).

   Several authors writing specifically about grief have noted the
importance of meaning in the resolution of grief. Marris considers
bereavement a process of change which can lead the bereaved into a new
sense of purpose about life; he believes that the context of meaning,

which helps the bereaved to develop new purposes, must be based on the fundamental structure of meaning which developed in childhood. It is through the struggle between one's past identity and conceptualizations about life and the present conflicts engendered by the loss that new viable interpretations about life and its meanings are reformulated (16). Cassem notes that loss and grief are indispensible to growth. He views bereavement as a continual process experienced throughout life. Cassem sees the ability to integrate misfortune into one's life in a positive, growth-producing manner as a mark of maturity. Thus prior maturity is probably the best predictor of who can negotiate the bereavement process and grow (12). Simos in her book on grief, indicates that suffering can be a force in providing life with meaning; however, for life to be tolerable after a loss, there must be an active search for the restoration of this meaning. This is first sought by addressing questions about the cause of death. Later, questions are addressed which attempt to find answers to the existential problem: "Why me? Why him?" Since the answers to these "why" questions may never be adequately answered, the bereaved are faced with the existential choice of how to deal with the resultant suffering (6). In his studies of survivors of holocaust and disaster, Lifton has noted two patterns of response. One pattern is that of numbing in which one's personal identity becomes constricted. The other, more positive response, is the struggle for rebirth/transformation in which new modes of being are sought through a complex process of personal change. This process may involve exploration, experimentation, and risk and is facilitated by support from others and by prior personal strengths (15).

Schneider has postulated a wholistic model of grief which attempts to integrate motivation for growth into the resolution of grief. The last phase, called "Transcending the Loss", represents the growth of the individual to no longer be bound by the power of what was lost or by attempts to rectify areas of personal vulnerability. Its purpose is to develop the capacity of the individual to extend beyond grief, to new commitments, balance, and wholeness in life (17). Like Schneider's model, Miles' conceptual model of parental grief includes a phase called the "Search for Meaning." The search at first involves an attempt to determine why the death occurred. Later, the search becomes deeper and more existential and involves deep profound questions about religion, self, life, and others. "Why me? Why my child? Where was God? How can life go on? What is my life all about?" Meaning may be found in: 1) adherence to religious and philosophical beliefs; 2) identification of the uniqueness of the child's life and death; 3) memorialization of the child's memory; or 4) becoming involved in activities that can help individuals and society. The search for meaning is hypothesized to ultimately affect the type of resolutions made to the child's death (19-20). The importance of the search for meaning in bereaved parents is supported by Craig who suggests that an essential part of the grief work of bereaved parents is the resolution of the meaninglessness of the crisis (18).

Methods

Since the concept of meaning and its ultimate impact on personal growth, especially within the framework of grief, is still under

development, it is difficult to know how it can be measured and studied.
Perhaps one method for beginning to evaluate the potential development
of meaning and personal growth in the lives of the bereaved is to look
at statements made by them about their experience. Information from
open-ended questions which asked bereaved parents in various ways to
describe themselves was examined in this descriptive analysis seeking
clues regarding both positive "growth" resolutions and negative
"despair" resolutions to the death of a child. The data were collected
in three separate studies which are part of an ongoing research program
on parental bereavement.

Findings

In the first study, 61 bereaved fathers responded to a mailed
questionnaire in which they were asked to respond to six open-ended
questions about their loss experience. In the last question they were
asked to list/discuss anything else about their grief which they wished
to share. Twenty-four fathers discussed their changed views about life
or their present perspective about how the loss affected them overall.
Of these twenty-four comments, nine indicated a positive resolution,
nine evidenced a more negative view of life, while the remainder
indicated that the father was still attempting to understand his loss or
else indicated some neutral statement. The positive responses included:
learning to prioritize and reorganize my goals, becoming more sensitive
and helpful to people who hurt, losing my fear of death, learning to
appreciate young people, and realizing the importance of spending more
time with my family. Negative responses tended to reflect the ideas
that life had stopped, that one will never get over it, and that no good
will ever come from the death.

In the second study, completed by Crandall and Miles (24) eight
bereaved fathers and thirty bereaved mothers were asked to complete a
20-Statement Questionnaire responding to the phrase "A Bereaved Mother
is..." or "A Bereaved Father is..." In content analysis of the data,
one of the major categories that emerged was "Bereavement Outcomes"
which included 29 percent of the mothers' 457 responses and 26 percent
of the fathers' 105 total responses. The data were further analyzed
into subcategories which included both positive and negative outcomes.
Positive outcome subcategories included: "Cherishing memories,"
"Feeling more positive about life," "Being more compassionate and more
caring of others," "Being more spiritual," and "Feeling stronger." The
positive outlook statements accounted for 40 percent of the responses of
mothers and 33 percent of the responses of fathers that were coded into
the "Bereavement Outcome" category. The negative outcome subcategories
included: "Not being able to forget or recover" and "Being unable to
resolve the loss." These accounted for 19 percent of the responses of
the mothers and 22 percent of the responses of the fathers coded into
the "Bereavement Outcome" category, a substantially smaller percentage
of responses than in the positive subcategories. The remainder of the
subcategories included statements that indicted that the parent was
still seeking answers and working toward recovery.

Specific comments of both mothers and fathers that were coded into
the positive subcategory of "Changed attitude about life" included some

of the following: grateful, more compassionate, more appreciative, more serious about life, more aware of the importance of other loved ones, aware of the fragility of life, and having a greater understanding of life and death. In another ongoing study of bereaved parents whose children died of chronic disease or sudden accidents, subjects were specifically asked to comment about their "Changed views about life." Of the numerous comments made by the 26 parents, 40 responses indicated a positive outlook, whereas only 13 responses were negative. Positive responses included: learning to live each day to the fullest, being more understanding of others who have experienced loss, feeling more loving toward others, having a stronger faith, being aware of the preciousness of life, and being a better person in general. Negative responses included: having a negative meaningless view of life, just existing, feeling suicidal, and lacking trust.

Discussion

The data presented here must be considered with caution because of the imprecise, indirect method of measuring meaning and growth. The parents studied were not directly asked about their search for meaning or about their potential growth as a result of their child's death. It was felt that directly asking parents these questions would bias their responses toward the negative pole, since bereaved parents are sensitive about the idea that growth could occur because of their child's death. In addition, the small convenience sample of parents who agreed to participate in these studies were, for the most part, members of a self-help group for bereaved parents. Parents who attend such groups may be a special group of individuals who differ in important ways from the general population of bereaved parents. For one thing, they are parents who are seeking help in their grief, and because of their attendance at a self-help group they may be more apt to find meaning and to grow. It should also be pointed out that the period of time since death was not considered in data analysis and may be an important factor in the evolution of the "Search for Meaning."

Nevertheless, it is interesting to note that so many of the comments given by these parents indicated that they had found some meaning and had grown in some important ways following the deaths of their children. The most commonly reported growth responses included being more compassionate and caring of others, especially the bereaved; having a stronger faith; and being aware of the preciousness and fragility of life which helped them live each day more fully. Additional clues about the potential for finding "meaning" in life following a child's death can be found in numerous newspaper clippings and magazine articles about bereaved parents who have started self-help groups, such as Compassionate Friends, and community action groups such as Mothers Against Drunken Drivers. Through such activities, these parents are making major contributions to society.

Focusing on the potential for "growth" resolution when a child has died is meant in no way to minimize the deep and long-lasting pain of grief which is experienced when a child has died. Rather, it is meant to point out the importance, as described by Frankl, of channelling the pain and rage into meaningful endeavors which can contribute to recovery and can assist society as well (13). Finally, research needs to focus more on this process of searching for meaning after the death of a loved one and on its potential for affecting the ultimate outcomes of grief in the bereaved. In addition, clinicians who are counseling the bereaved need to be aware of the importance of helping grieving clients deal with the existential search for meaning in their loss.

REFERENCES

1. Shneidman, E. Voices of Death. New York: Harper and Row, 1980.

2. Balkwell, C. Transition to Widowhood: A Review of the Literature.
   Family Relations, 1981, 30, 117-127.

3. Clayton, P.J., Halikes, J.A., & Maurice, W.L. The Bereavement of
   the Widowed. Diseases of the Nervous System, 1971, 32(9),
   597-604.

4. Parkes, C.M. Bereavement: Studies of Grief in Adult Life. London:
   International Universities Press, 1972.

5. Sanders, C.M. Comparison of Young and Older Spouses in Bereavement
   Outcomes. Omega, 1980-1981, 11(3), 217-232.

6. Simos, B.G. A Time to Grieve: Loss as a Universal Human
   Experience. New York: Family Service Association of America,
   1979.

7. Clayton, P.J. Mortality and Morbidity in the First Year of Widowhood. Archives of General Psychiatry, 1974, 30, 749-750.

8. Kraus, A.L., & Lilienfield, A.M. Some Epidemiological Aspects of
   the High Mortality Rate in the Young Widowed Group.
   Journal of Chronic Diseases, 1959, 10, 207-217.

9. Maddison, D., & Walker, W.L. Factors Affecting the Outcome of
   Conjugal Bereavement. British Journal of Psychiatry, 1967,
   113, 1057-1067.

10. Parkes, C.M. Determinants of Outcome Following Bereavement. Omega,
    1975, 6, 303-323.

11. Young, M., Benjamin, B., & Walis, C. Mortality of Widowers.
    Lancet, 1963, 2, 454-456.

12. Cassem, N.H. Bereavement as Indispensable for Growth. In
    Schoenberg, B., Gerber, I., Weiner, A. et al (Eds.)
    Bereavement: Its Psychosocial Aspects. New York: Columbia
    University Press, 1975, p. 9-17.

13. Frankl, V.E. Man's Search for Meaning. New York: Simon and
    Schuster, 1963.

14. Koestenbaum, P. Is There an Answer to Death? Englewood Cliffs,
    N.J.: Prentice-Hall, 1976.

15. Lifton, R.J. & Olson, E. Living and Dying. New York: Praeger
    Publishers, 1974.

16. Marris, P. Loss and Change. New York: Pantheon Books, 1974.

17. Frears, L.H., & Schneider, J.M. Exploring Grief and Loss in a
    Wholistic Framework. Personnel and Guidance Journal, 1981,
    59(6), 341-345.

18. Craig, Y. The Bereavement of Parents and Their Search for Meaning.
    British Journal of Social Work, 1977, 7(1), 41-54.

19. Miles, M.S. The Grief of Parents: A Model for Assessment and
    Intervention. Unpublished paper presented at the Annual
    Conference, Forum for Death Education and Counseling, Orlando,
    FLorida, 1979.

20. Miles, M.S. Helping Adults Mourn the Death of a Child. In Wass, H.
    & Corr, C. (Eds.) Childhood and Death. New York: Hemisphere
    Publishing, 1984.

21. Gunther, J. Death Be Not Proud. New York: Harper and Row, 1949.

22. Hill, R. Generic Features of Families Under Stress. In Parad,
    H.J., (Ed.) Crisis Intervention: Selected Readings. New York:
    Family Service Association of America, 1965, p. 32-52.

23. McCubbin, H.I, Joy, C.B., Cauble, A.E., et al. Family Stress and
    Coping: A Decade Review. Journal of Marriage and the Family,
    1980, 42(4), 855-871.

24. Crandall, E.K.B. Grieving Fathers and Mothers: Their Self-Concepts.
    Unpublished Master's Thesis, University of Kansas, 1982.

A DEATH IN THE FAMILY: LONG-TERM IMPACT

ON THE LIFE OF THE FAMILY

Patricia A. Hyland

Introduction: "The knowledge that because of her age my
mother's life must soon come to an end
did not lessen the horrible surprise."

(1, p. 108)

The death of a loved one often presents severe stress for the individual and the family. Like working through any stressful time the process can be adaptive or maladaptive. The surviving members will go on to pursue a successful life or they will suffer symptoms and not fulfill their individual potential. In the past as a nurse I have had occasion to work directly with dying persons and their immediate available family members. In my present position as a social worker, although I am not directly involved with the dying or with the immediate impact of death on the survivors, I continue to be struck by the long-term impact of loss on some individuals and their families. In some families significant losses have occurred years previously but have not been adequately dealt with or resolved, and maladaptive patterns have developed. These patterns often lead to psychological symptoms in individuals which lead to referrals for help from the families involved.

The purpose of this paper is to examine, with the aid of examples from clinical case histories, the influence of past loss on present understanding and treatment of families with members who have developed psychological symptoms. In spite of abundant literature on the subject of death and dying, little attention has been paid to the long-term effects that death of a family member can have on the entire family system. A detailed history, paying attention to past deaths in the family system, can help lead to resolution of a variety of presenting symptoms. What initially appears to be unexplainable behavior on the part of one family member can then be understood as a residue or aborted grief reaction. With assistance, resolutions can then occur, resulting in a decrease of the presenting symptoms.

I have chosen case examples from my work with families during my last three years working in the field of social work. These specific examples were chosen to illustrate how death at varying stages in the life cycle of the family can affect not only individuals but the family unit as a whole, and how symptoms of one individual can often be "protective" for other family members.

Case Example #1: Following the Death of a Neonate

A couple of years ago Brian, a nine-year-old boy, was brought for evaluation to a community agency where I worked. His presenting difficulties included hyperactivity, inability to obey rules and structure at home and at school, and complaints that he often acted as a much younger child. Family history revealed that Brian had been adopted. It was also learned that his parents had two older natural siblings and that his adoptive mother had delivered a stillborn infant two years prior to Brian's adoption. Following the stillborn birth a hysterectomy was performed on the mother for medical reasons. When Brian was adopted at ten months of age his name was changed "to fit in with the rest of the family." Although some of Brian's symptomatology could be understood due to the history prior to his adoption, subsequent changes in his behavior did not begin to occur until the parents were able to mourn their stillborn infant and view Brian separately as their adopted son who could not replace the infant they had previously lost. Over time, communications between the parents became more open and they began to resolve some of the longstanding feelings that had been unrecognized and not dealt with prior to this time.

Approximately one-third of all pregnant women do not end up with a baby; some of these women lose their infants in the first few months of life. The pain for the mother and/or parents at the loss of an infant or unborn child can be excruciating. It is not uncommon for parents who have suffered such a loss to avoid sharing feelings with one another. Communication between the parents can then break down and over time can become more and more difficult. Poor communication can lead to anger, suppression of feelings, guilt, self-doubt, and loss of confidence in oneself and in one's spouse. When the repressed feelings are not resolved, they can continue to fester, leading to further hurt and angry feelings. In this context future pregnancies are planned often to replace the lost child. This can lead to future problems for the unborn child as well as for his parents (2, p. 13-20).

Brian's parents had not only unsuccessfully mourned the infant's death but following that they had been unable to deal openly with their feelings around their inability to have more natural children of their own. Their inability to successfully resolve their grief reactions following the death of their infant led them, in part, to the adoption of Brian. He later developed symptoms, and these were not resolved until his parents were able to work through their own grief at the loss of their infant.

Case Example #2:   <u>Following the Death of a Spouse</u>

I met Mrs. M. several months ago. She had been instrumental in bringing in her adolescent niece for treatment because of depression and suicidal ideation. Initially it was somewhat confusing that the referral came from the adolescent's aunt rather than from her parents. It was then learned that the niece had been living with her aunt. Her parents, who lived only thirty miles away, had been unable to control their daughter's behavior. History revealed that Mrs. M.'s husband had died unexpectedly three years previously. Although Mrs. M. had two children, ages two and one-half and six, she had attempted to assist her niece as well as several other family members, at various times since her husband had died. Mrs. M. also suffered from asthma and although this had been a problem most of her life, she stated that her attacks had gotten considerably worse since she was widowed. During the past year, Mrs. M. had been hospitalized on several occasions for pneumonia.

As I talked to Mrs. M. it became apparent to me that she had avoided many of her own grief reactions and avoided adjusting to her new life as a single parent by taking care of others. Her own feelings could be avoided as she helped other family members deal with theirs. When caring for others became too stressful, Mrs. M. developed physical symptoms and hospitalization served to meet some of the unmet needs that Mrs. M. herself experienced. Over the last several months Mrs. M. had come to realize that helping her niece had become too difficult for her both emotionally and physically. Although she often felt lonely when someone else was not in her home, Mrs. M. felt that she should start to concentrate on herself and her children so that they could experience a more stable life. I agreed with Mrs. M. and strongly supported her decision to allow her niece's parents to take over her care. We talked at length about her husband's death and how difficult it had been for her to readjust following this loss. I further supported Mrs. M.'s own need for support in her new role as a single parent with two young children. Following these interactions, Mrs. M. became more regularly involved in the counseling process she had started prior to contacting our agency. For the last several months she has been able to avoid rescuing others (now she only offers advice), and has been able to avoid hospitalization for several months. I met Mrs. M.'s children briefly only once and although no behavior difficulties had been noted I would suspect that her children are enjoying the benefits of having a mother who is at home more and they do not have to suffer from continued separation due to their mother's hospitalizations.

There are approximately ten million widowed men and women in the United States. Approximatley eight hundred and fifty thousand individuals join the ranks of the widowed each year (3, p. 267). For most of these people the loss of their spouse is unpredictable, and therefore a major and difficult life event. Among other things they are faced with loneliness, reduced income, loss of companionship including unmet sexual needs, and a lack of comfort and support previously provided by the partner. Some widows or widowers also experience an increase in physical problems or concerns following the death of their spouse. In an article entitled "The Grieving Spouse" (4), Greenblott describes four stages a spouse must go through before resolving the partner's death: stage one - shock, numbness, denial, and disbelief (this can last for a few days to many months); stage two - characterized by pining, yearning, and depression (lasting from five to fourteen days to the remainder of one's life); stage three - the period of emancipation from the loved one and readjustment to a new environment (usually beginning after six to eight weeks, but for some it is not completed or begun for years); and stage four, which involves identity reconstruction or the crystallization of new relationships and the development of a new role in life without a partner.

Following the loss of a spouse it seems most typical for friends and relatives to tolerate and support grief feelings only for a short time, i.e., the first two months after the death has occurred. After that the bereaved person is usually left more or less alone to deal with the feelings of loss. Unfortunately, this occurs at the time when suppport is most needed. When dependent children are also involved in the grieving process, it is a source of concern to note that the parent without sufficient support cannot provide the necessary support to his or her grieving dependent children.

When I met Mrs. M. she had been unsuccessful in her readjustment as a single parent. She had avoided resolving her painful feelings around her husband's death. Helping her to recognize and discuss this helped Mrs. M. to begin a more successful readjustment for herself and her children to a new more stable life style.

Case Example #3: Following the Death of a Parent

Several months ago, Mark was referred for an inpatient psychiatric evaluation at our facility. At that time he was fourteen years of age, the youngest of two brothers. His presenting symptoms included abuse of illicit drugs, defiant and uncontrollable behavior in the home and at school, and occasional angry outbursts particularly directed toward his mother. History revealed that his paternal grandmother (an extended family member who had always lived in the family home) had died when Mark was nine and one-half years of age. When Mark was eleven his father was diagnosed as having cancer and died one year later. Both deaths were viewed by the remaining family members as "the will of God" and few feelings were shared in the family around either of these very painful losses. During Mark's father's illness, his older brother and mother often visited his father in the hospital. Mark's age and the hospital regulations made it difficult for Mark to go very often. It was also thought by the family to be less painful and more normal for a boy his age to be out with friends. This was a very difficult time for Mark and his family, and his occasional use of marijuana and defiance of rules at home went unnoticed. Few sad or angry feelings were expressed and on the surface it looked like the family was adjusting fairly well to the loss of the father. In reality Mark's behavior continued to deteriorate. One year later, he was admitted to a psychiatric hospital because of the above mentioned symptoms.

The family members could make no connection between the father's and grandmother's deaths and Mark's difficulties of the past year. Psychiatric evaluation revealed that the mourning process had barely begun for Mark and for his family, and in fact, their feelings concerning their grandmother's and father's deaths had been pushed asided and avoided. Mark's conflicts and difficulties partially served to divert the focus from the very painful grief reactions the individual family members had yet to work through.

A study done by Ewalt and Perkins in 1979 (5) revealed that one out of every hundred students had suffered the loss of a parent. When a child or adolescent loses a parent, feelings can be profound and very painful. If these are not adequately dealt with, unresolved feelings and conflicts can lead to dysfunctional individual behavior and to the development of maladaptive family patterns.

Following the death of a loved one an adolescent can regress to more infantile behavior. Denial among adolescents is a common element. Other reactions include egocentrism, magical thinking, rage, and at times extreme dependency. Usually with much emotional support and an opportunity to verbalize concern and clarify misconceptions, adolescents can over time adjust to their loss (6, pp. 18-23).

Mark's reactions over time developed into psychiatric symptoms. He developed dependency on drugs and rage, along with other symptoms. Understanding the impact of the loss of his father on Mark individually, along with understanding of the family dynamics, involved helping Mark and his family to begin to reorganize their family structure in an adaptive way--a task that prior to that time had not been possible for Mark or his family.

Case Example #4:   Following the Death of an Older Parent or Grandparent

Judy, a fifteen-year-old only child, was brought for treatment because she refused to attend school on a regular basis, and was failing in all of her high school subjects. History revealed that three of her four grandparents were deceased. They had died within a three-year period; her paternal grandfather had been the last to die two years previously. Judy's father was also an only child. A more detailed history of presenting symptoms revealed that Judy began missing school occasionally prior to her paternal grandfather's death. THis was not seen as serious and she was able to keep up with her school work until three months ago, when the beloved family pet dog died suddenly and unexpectedly. At this point Judy's symptomatology increased. The grandparents' deaths were seen as normal and expected, and minimal feelings were expressed in the family around these losses. The loss of the believed pet was seen as cruel and unfair, and extremely painful feelings were expressed by each family member. It soon became apparent that while their pet had been very important and considerably missed, some of their unresolved feelings around the grandparents' deaths had been expressed when their dog died. As Judy's parents were able to further express and come to terms with their own feelings concerning the loss of their parents, the reactions to the loss of their pet lessened and Judy was able to begin attending school on a more regular basis.

An older person is expected at some time to die, and this is considered natural and normal. Yet, if the elderly person who dies is our grandparent or our own parent, individuals can often be initially surprised by their very strong reactions to their own personal loss. These feelings can be denied and not faced. In our society miles and busy life styles often separate the family generations and most people do not participate in the final stages of parents' or grandparents' lives. This can, for many, lead to unresolved feelings and conflicts that can surface and then become troublesome for years, and can even affect relationships with children and younger generations.

"The meaning of the loss of a parent is often largely internal and symbolic...death of a parent marks the end of one's oldest relationship and affects one's relationship with survivors. The idea that even after healthy adjustment the organization has accomplished there is always some residual loss to be mourned and growth to be achieved." (7, p. 1155).

Judy's symptoms became more understandable as the family history was taken and explored. Judy's parents had been unprepared to become the oldest surviving members in their family. Painful unresolved feelings around the loss of Judy's grandparents, particularly for the parents, could be avoided by Judy's developing symptoms. Dealing with these unresolved grief reactions allowed Judy's parents to again allow Judy to attend school. She no longer needed to help her parents with their grief work.

Discussion

Death of a loved one, for some families, can lead to the development of psychiatric symptoms in individual family members. It has been my experience that a detailed history, paying particular attention to deaths in each family, can lead to increased understanding of why the symptoms developed and what purpose those same symptoms may serve in the family. Once these dynamics are understood reorganization of the family in a more adaptive way is often possible. Professionals need to be aware of the possibility of maladaptive patterns developing in individuals in the service of their families. The earlier the abnormal reactions can be recognized, the easier it might be to direct the individual and his or her family back on the road to more adaptive functioning, thus avoiding painful psychiatric symptoms.

By the same token the longer the interval between the unresolved loss and the family presenting for help, the more obscure the symptoms will be, as derivatives of the earlier loss. More work will have to be done to discover the various connections between the current symptomatic picture and the earlier loss. It is my experience that despite these difficulties, effective bereavement can be achieved. In the timeless unconscious the effects of death can remain very much alive despite the variety of psychological maneuvers the individual and family make to keep the effects of the loss concealed.

> "When someone you love dies, you pay for
> the sin of outliving her with a thousand
> piercing regrets."
>   (1, p. 108).

References

1. DeBeauvoir, Simone. A Very Easy Death. New York: Warner Books, 1964.

2. Peppers, Larry G., & Knapp, Ronald J. Motherhood and Mourning: Perinatal Death. New York: Praeger Publishers, 1980.

3. Prichard, L., et al. (eds.) Social Work with the Dying Patient and the Family. New York: Columbia University Press, 1977.

4. Greenblott, M.A. The Grieving Spouse. American Journal of Psychiatry, 1978, 135(1), 43-52.

5. Ewalt, Patricia L., & Perkins, Lola A. The Real Experience of Death Among Adolescents: An Empirical Study. University of Kansas, Lawrence, April 1979 (Unpublished paper).

6. Sahler, Olle Jane Z. The Child and Death. St. Louis, Mo.: C.V. Mosby, 1978.

7. Malinak, M.A., Dennis, P., et al. Adult Reactions to the Death of a Parent: A Preliminary Study. American Journal of Psychology, 1979, 136(9), 1152-1156.

Bibliography

Boyer, Kathleen B. The Amish Way of Death: A Study of Family Support
    Systems. American Psychologist, 1979, 34, 255-261.

Carey, Raymond G. The Widowed, A Year Later. Counseling Psychology,
    1977, 24(2), 125-131.

Cohen, Pauline, et al. Family Adaption to Terminal Illness and Death
    of a Parent. Social Casework, 1977, ___, 223-228.

Embleton, Leota. Children, Cancer, and Death: a Discussion of a Support
    Core System. Canada's Mental Health, 1979, 27(4), 12-15.

Furman, E.F. A Child's Parent Dies., New Haven, Conn.: Yale University
    Press, 1974.

Hardt, Dale Vincent. An Investigation of the Stages of Bereavement.
    Omega, 1978-79, 9(3), 279-286.

Hare-Mustin, Rachel, T. Family Therapy Following the Death of a
    Child. Journal of Marital and Family Therapy, 1979, 5(2), 151-159.

Johnson, Jay, & Johnson, S.M. Children Die Too. Des Moines, Ia.:
    Centering Corporation, 1978.

Kaffman, Mordecai, & Elizur, Esther. Children's Breavement Reactions
    Following Death of the Father. International Journal of Family
    Therapy, 1979, 1(3), 203-229.

Krell, Robert, & Robken, Leslie. The Effects of Sibling Death on the
    Surviving Child: A Family Perspective. Family Process, 1979,
    18(4), 471-477.

Kubler-Ross, Elisabeth. On Death and Dying. New York: Macmillan
    Publishing Co., 1969.

Kubler-Ross, Elisabeth. Death: The Final Stage of Growth. Englewood
    Cliffs, N.J.: Prentice-Hall, 1975.

Kutscher, Austin H. Death and Bereavement. Springfield, Ill.: Banner-
    stone House, 1969.

LeShan, Eda. Learning to Say Goodbye: When a Parent Dies. New York:
    Macmillan, 1976.

Schoenburg, B., et al. (eds.) Anticipatory Grief. New York: Columbia
    University Press, 1979.

Solomon, Michael A., & Hursch, L. Brian. Death in the Family:
    Implications for Family Development. Journal of Marital and Family
    Therapy, 1979, 5(2), 43-50.

Towley, Kay. The Choice of a Surviving Sibling as 'Scapegoat' in Some Cases of Maternal Bereavement: A Case Report. Journal of Child Psychology and Psychiatry, 1975, 16, 337-339.

EXPLORING PARANORMAL EXPERIENCES OF THE BEREAVED

Bonnie Lindstrom

Abraham Lincoln has been seen walking the halls of the White House after his death...The ghost of Dolly Madison has been seen in the Rose Garden she planted at the White House, keeping the gardeners from digging it up...The garden remains to this day. Stories like this abound in lore and literature.

This paper will go a step further and examine the kinds of "ghost-like" or paranormal experiences that are a natural, normal phenomena of grief following the loss of a loved one. I have defined a paranormal experience as one in which the overwhelming intuitive or sensory presence of a deceased loved one is felt by the bereaved person.

In my almost six years of counseling families as part of a hospice bereavement follow-up program, I have become fascinated by the experiences families have shared with me. Through both clinical experience and data gathered from a general survey questionnaire given to families thirteen months after their loss, we have found that more than half of the families we work with have had such an experience. I will discuss these phenomena and their relationship to the bereaved and those working with them.

Studies done by Colin Murray Parkes (1) and W. Dewi Rees (2) document the occurrence of hallucinations in the bereaved. In a 1971 study Rees interviewed 227 widows and 66 widowers in mid-Wales. His results showed that 46.7 percent had post bereavement hallucinations and that they often lasted many years. Earlier surveys of London widows by Parkes yielded similar results. Both Parkes and Rees acknowledged that the hallucinations were usually quite comforting. Rees reported them as more common when the marriages were happy and had produced children. He found no correlation in sex, race, or religion. Neither Parkes nor Rees made any attempt to interpret these experiences as anything but a normal psychological symptom of bereavement.

In his major works, Attachment and Loss (3), John Bowlby discusses the feelings of presence that a survivor experiences. He describes them as a normal symptom of the phase of yearning and searching for the lost loved one. He also explores the cross-cultural nature of these experiences which seem to occur in almost all societies and are seen as a positive happening in most.

Thelma Moss, a medical psychologist at UCLA's Neuropsychiatric Institute, has done research in the area of parapsychology (4). Dr. Moss suggests the possibility that there may exist an energy body, or etheric body. This body may sometimes leave the physical body. She poses the question of what might become of the energy body at death. Are these the cause of paranormal experiences?

In his doctoral dissertation (5), Wistar McLaren interviewed six individuals who felt a continued relationship with their deceased loved one via intuitive paranormal experiences. Each of them found the experience comforting, offering hope for continuity of life.

Rosalind Heywood is a prominent English authority on psychical research. She writes, "modern ghosts seem usually to want to help, or warn, or merely to appear to a loved friend or relative. And sometimes they are not distinguished from living persons until they vanish" (6, p. 376). She also states that at the present time it entails "an act of faith" to look at the possibility of survival after death.

In the following paragraphs, I will describe how these paranormal phenomena have been experienced by bereaved persons in our hospice program. I have divided them into six categories: intuitive, visual, auditory, olfactory, tactile, and dreams.

An <u>intuitive</u> experience involves an overwhelming sense of presence, a "knowing that one is not alone." These "intuitive" experiences are by far the most common.

One person stated: "First at the funeral, I had a warm peaceful feeling, comforting. I knew it was my mother. Many times I have these feelings, however I cannot create them on my own. Just like in life, this feeling comes to me when my mother feels I need her. Sometimes I've wanted it but have to face things on my own."

Another said: "I was very comforted. At first, I doubted it was her, after a while I was positive it was her."

<u>Visual</u> experiences are less common, but very powerful. The deceased usually appears well and often has a comforting, peaceful facial expression. Visions, more than the other paranormal awarenesses can lead one to fear their own sanity. However, in all cases related to me the survivors have been deeply rooted in reality and certainly knew it would not be in their best interest to broadcast the experiences to friends and relatives. A woman who admitted to having had psychotic hallucinations told me that when her husband died and she saw him in a vision she distinctly knew the difference between that experience and her previous hallucinations. Following are two examples.

I awakened suddenly with the feeling Harry was there. And I saw him standing at the foot of my bed, smiling, and he said, "Don't worry, Anna, everything will be o.k. The boys will help and I know you are capable. Love conquers all, love one another."

Another said: "One night I was sitting on the bed, my wife peeked around the corner like she used to. I saw her."

In <u>auditory</u> experiences survivors often hear the person who has died call their name. Following are two examples of other auditory experiences.

One person said: "I have heard her footsteps

walking through the house."

Another related: "I woke up in the middle of the night
to go to the bathroom. When I went back to bed, I could
hear his breathing, very heavy. I felt as if he was trying
to tell me he was alright, really saying goodbye. I believe
it was his spirit. I believe he was telling me he was
alright and happy."

Over the last few years, a few people have described to me a paranormal experience involving the sense of smell. An <u>olfactory</u> experience
usually involves the odor of a loved one's perfume or aftershave lotion.
The following is a more unusual experience:

We could all smell her colostomy bag around the house
for two or three weeks. The smell was definitely not
there the first month or so after her death.

The sense of <u>touch</u> may be the rarest of paranormal phenomena in the
bereaved. Several survivors have shared that they felt a hug or
familiar caress, often very shortly after death in a "saying goodbye."

<u>Dreams</u> of the departed are a common, almost universal, occurrence
in grief. Sometimes these are repetitive in nature, perhaps symbolizing
a sense of "unfinished business." A young woman I recently worked with
lost her husband in a plane crash and was not permitted to view his
body. This was a major source of conflict for her as she feels she
never said goodbye and has not accepted his death. She dreams repeti-
tively of his coming home and telling her it was all a mistake, that he
had been with his brother in Alaska all the time.

Other survivors feel they are visited by their loved ones in
dreams.

One woman wrote: "While I've had many dreams about him,
only a couple have felt like he was really <u>there</u> and not
just a part of the dream. In those few dreams I felt I
worked out many changes in my own grief and recovery."

The previous six types of experiences may occur at different times
for the same individual or in some persons simultaneously. In my
clinical experience, most visions occur in the evening though all
experiences can occur anywhere and at any time of day.

Perhaps most fascinating of all are those paranormal phenomena
shared by more than one person simultaneously. Following a presentation
at a workshop on bereavement where we discussed these events, I received
a letter from a participant which contained the following remarks:

My sister died in November, 1972. The following
summer her husband came to the lake to spend a few
days with us. He and Nora had been at the lake with
us a few years past—they had always taken camping
vacations—loved to camp and fish—and had a tent and

other equipment. This particular time, Jim had the tent.
As we were unfolding it and getting ready to put it up,
he and I had a very strong sense of Nora's presence. It
was almost like I should be able to reach out and touch
her. Jim was unnerved by the experience and decided he'd
sleep in the back of his station wagon rather than put up
the tent. Both of us, in talking about the experience
later, were amazed at how strong her presence was—there
was no feeling of fear—only the sharing of a common
experience we had so often shared before.

I have found the intuitive experience to be a common <u>shared</u> event,
however, shared visions and other paranormal phenomena are <u>not</u> unusual.

Here I would like to discuss the feelings or emotional states
aroused in survivors who have had a paranormal experience. Most have
told me that they truly believe it was the spirit of their loved one
coming back to reassure them and give encouragement to go on. Some
state the experience was wonderful, but acknowledge that they created it
through "wishful thinking" or imagination. The feelings commonly
associated with the experience are positive. Survivors most often
describe feelings of comfort, peace, warmth, and happiness. Statements
such as "I feel I'm never alone", "It's a way of communicating", and "I
felt he was absolutely there", are usual. Occasionally someone will
experience an initial fright at the experience. This fear is usually
transient and quickly replaced by another, more positive affective
state.

In many survivors, the paranormal experience has a profound impact
on their bereavement journey. Often as a part of the event, they
perceive a message to go on with their lives and that their beloved is
in "a good place" and being well cared for. The message is usually
reassuring to the survivor who may then feel ready to build a new life.

A dramatic example of this is the case of an elderly woman whose
50-year marriage ended when her husband died of a brain tumor. She
became morose, helpless, isolated from others, and bitter, seeing no
hope for any joy in her life. About five months after his death, as I
arrived for a home visit, she ran out to the driveway crying, "He came
back, he came back!" A few nights previous to this she had awakened to
see him sitting next to her bed, looking well, as before his illness.
She felt he was reassuring her and telling her to go on. The healing in
this woman's grief was sudden and dramatic. She became hopeful and
outgoing again.

Freud (7) has written about some potential dangers in these experiences. His primary concern relates to the individual maintaining an
ongoing internal relationship with the deceased, thereby avoiding the
creation of new relationships and the letting go of the lost love
object. I have not seen this occur. In fact, more often the survivor
senses a permission to reach out and develop new relationships in a new
life.

Paranormal events seem to ameliorate the pain, diminish the sense of aloneness, and for many create a new sense of peace and hopefulness with God and the continuity of life.

The role of the counselor with the client who has had such an experience is relatively simple. As in all counseling relationships, an attitude of warmth and acceptance must prevail before the survivor will even reveal his or her paranormal experience. Because of my personal interest in this area, I usually ask directly by saying something like: "...during their grief, many people experience events that are unexplainable. Some actually feel the presence of or see the person who has died. This is quite normal. Have you ever had an experience like this?"

This opens the door and survivors often feel a great sense of relief in sharing and realizing they are not "crazy." Some individuals feel somehow that by sharing their experience it will lose its uniqueness or specialness for them. They should not be pressured. In the context of the counseling session it is important to: offer reassurance and acceptance of the experience; assist them in concretizing the experience through review; and help them to clarify its meaning for themselves. In a very few cases, it is necessary through psychiatric history to ascertain that more strange and frightening experiences are not symptomatic of a serious psychiatric disorder. In my experience, these are rare.

It is my strong opinion that no interpretation of the psychological or spiritual significance of the paranormal experience should be made by the counselor. The counselor should only guide the survivors in their own search for a comfortable explanation, which may mean that no explanation is at all necessary.

The potential for research in this area is limited only by the reluctance of credible, established professionals to venture into such an esoteric direction. Those who do are often ridiculed and their work not accepted by their peers. However, in recent years, a few highly regarded journals such as The American Journal of Psychiatry and the American Psychologist have published articles dealing with such things as near-death experiences.

Research in the area of the paranormal experiences related here should not seek to "prove" anything, but only to observe and document the phenomenon and its perceived meaning and impact.

Some areas where research would be helpful to our understanding of this phenomenon include:

1) Looking at bereavement outcomes in relationship to the occurrence of paranormal phenomena.

2) A study of the relationship of these phenomena to various personality variables and life experiences.

3) An exploration, on a longitudinal basis, of the meaning of

these experiences to the survivor and whether their perception of the experience changes over time.

In this chapter, I have attempted to describe an experience almost universal in the bereaved. I have not proposed, and will not offer, any explanation for these events. Each individual must come to their personal meaning based on their approach to life, relationships, and their own spirituality. One cannot argue that a continued relationship with our loved ones after death, whether spiritual or psychological, is a hopeful, comforting concept.

Out of love, we create love.

REFERENCES

1. Parkes, C.M. The First Year of Bereavement: A Longitudinal Study of the Reaction of London Widows to the Death of Their Husbands. Psychiatry, 1970, 33, 444-467.

2. Rees, W. Dewi. The Bereaved and Their Hallucinations. In B. Schoenberg, et al. (eds.), Bereavement: Its Psychosocial Aspects. New York: Columbia University Press, 1975, pp. 66-71.

3. Bowlby, J. Attachment and Loss, Vol. III, Loss. New York: Basic Books, 1980.

4. Moss, T. The Probability of the Impossible. New York: New American Library, 1974.

5. MacLaren, W. The Deceased Other: Presence and Absence. A dissertation presented to the faculty of the California School of Professional Psychology, July, 1980.

6. Haywood, R. Death and Psychical Research: The Present Position Regarding the Evidence of Survival. In E.S. Shneidman (ed.), Death: Current Perspectives. 2nd ed.; Palo Alton, Ca.: Mayfield Publishing Co., 1980, pp. 375-378.

7. Freud, S. Mourning and Melancholia, The Standard Edition of Complete Psychological Works of Sigmund Freud. (Vol. 14) London: Hogarth Press, 1957.

SECTION FOUR

CREATIVITY IN DEATH EDUCATION

SECTION FOUR

CREATIVITY IN DEATH EDUCATION

Death education as a widespread and reasonably respectable phenomenon in North American academic can hardly be said to be more than 10 or 15 years old--barely an adolescent in human developmental terms. At the time of the Forum's founding, this genre of educational activity in all of its many forms was the subject of burgeoning growth and innovation. Now it has settled a bit into various recognizable patterns. Consequently, there is new opportunity for additional reflection and criticism. In this Section, we provide two pieces, rather different in character, each of which contributes its own element of creativity to the overall field.

In Chapter 12, Shirley Scott traces the origins and structure of her own continuing education programs and a full-scale course on death education for nurses and nursing students. Scott would be the first to acknowledge that this is not wholly unprecedented or unparalleled work. But her account is a good example of how a sensitive and sensible person can first teach herself enough about the content of a sector of our field and enough about practical pedagogy to be able then to turn to the instruction of others. Indeed, Scott is quite clear that much of the learning in such contexts is accomplished jointly, with all of the participants contributing their own proper share. This is "creativity in the trenches", innovation at the front-line level which will be most appreciated by those who experience it.

Another sort of creativity calls for reflection on that which becomes almost habitual in our teaching practices. In Chapter 13, the example is the opening exercises so often employed to introduce workshops and courses in death education. Charles and Donna Corr first describe such experiences so as to make clear the scope of their concern. They then raise issues about compliance within such exercises, their ostensive content, and the interpretation of their results. The point is to provoke reflection on the care that we need to take in subjecting people to exercises in this subject area, on their purported significance, and on the value of the exercise process itself when rightly understood and employed. In part, the larger issue here has to do with the overall goals of death education in most of its forms. To raise topics of this sort is to foster creativity in death education and counseling in ways that we hope have permeated this entire volume and the larger work of the Forum for Death Education and Counseling.

DEATH EDUCATION FOR NURSES: PARTS I AND II

Shirley Scott

Death education for nurses and nursing students is becoming more widely recognized as a necessary part of their professional preparation.

Over the past several years I have drawn on my experience as an oncology nurse, hospice nurse, counselor, and nursing instructor to develop and teach death education courses specifically designed for continuing education programs for registered nurses and licensed practical nurses. These courses have been well attended by nurses of all ages and lengths of nursing experience. Following each of the presentations I asked the participants to write down their answers to two questions: "In what way(s) did this program help you feel more comfortable caring for a dying person?", and "What topic would you like to haved discussed in a future death related program?" The answers given indicated that not only did all the death education topics need to be covered, but the nurses also wanted information and skills which would enable them to deal effectively with the diverse and changing needs of terminally ill patients.

I first became aware that many nurses wanted this type of information when I was working as a hospice nurse. Whenever I was with a group of nurses (such as at conferences and continuing education programs) and mentioned that I was working for a hospice, there was always a barrage of questions about how I did my job. "What do you say to a person when he asks you, 'Am I dying'?" "What can you do when is person is so angry about everything and is taking it out on the nurses and everyone in sight?" "How can you work only with dying people all the time?" "How do you control severe pain without completely zonking the patient?" I tried to give bits of helpful information in the limited time available during lunch and other breaks. It was obvious by the number of people who gathered around at these times that there was a real need for further discussion of these topics.

After several such encounters (and spurred on by one comment of "I wish you were giving a workshop on these things today!"), I developed a two- hour program entitled "Caring for the Terminally Ill Patient." This was first presented to nurses in two small hospitals for a total of about 40 people. Included in this program were a brief discussion of death denial in this country, a death awareness exercise, discussion of the emotional stages terminally ill people may experience, and some ways nurses can help people cope with these emotions. The basic concepts of comfort and care, and effective pain and symptom control were also included. Questions from the audience brought forth other concerns which could be addressed only briefly--the fear of being with a person at the time of death and not knowing what to expect; fear of administering large doses of narcotics routinely around the clock; ambiguous feelings about ethical and moral issues; frustration about not having enough time to stay with the dying person.

In answering the questionnaire at the close of each program, the nurses stated other concerns and needs. One stated, "I'm so afraid of death myself I could hardly stand to hear you talk about it at first. But right now I feel I would like more opportunity to talk about death and dying and try to get myself more comfortable so I could be of some help to my patients." Another wrote, "I'd like to know more about communicating with both the terminally ill and their family members— how to help them all make the most of the time the patient has left."

After analyzing the questionnaires from the first two presentations it was obvious to me that a few two- hour programs could not possibly cover all the material nurses wanted to learn! I sketched out a course of study which would include both the death education and nursing topics which had been suggested. I discovered the course would have to be at least 28 to 30 hours in length in order to cover all the material, give participants a chance to assimilate the information, discuss the pros and cons, practice the communication skills with each other, and begin to make the new knowledge a part of their everyday thinking. Unfortunately, an opportunity was not available to me at that time to present such a lengthy course.

My best alternative was to accept the challenge to work out a number of presentations which would fit into the format of the Valencia Community College Continuing Education for Nurses schedule. These could be two, three, or six-hour programs, but there was still the problem of scheduling a series and, of course, no way to be sure the same people would sign up for all the related courses.

Over a period of months I developed and taught the following series of related programs which were offered individually:

Death and Dying - a 3-hour introduction to death education.
Overcoming Fears Related to Caring for Dying Patients - 3 hours
Comfortable Communication with Terminally Ill Patients and Their Families - 6 hours
Caring for the Terminally Ill Patient and Yourself - 3 hours
Effective Pain and Symptom Control for Terminally Ill Patients - 2 hours
Meeting the Needs of the Cancer Patient - 6 hours
Hospice Care for the Terminally Ill - 2 hours
Loss and Grief - 3 hours

Some of the same material was incorporated in all of the programs which enabled the participants to learn about some of the basic death education topics even if they attended only one of the series.

During a two- year period these programs were repeated a number of times as part of the Valencia Community College series in Continuing Education for Nurses. Several were also sponsored by local nursing groups and other community colleges in the area. At the conclusion of each program, I asked the participants to fill out the same two-part questionnaire. The answers I got back corroborated the information given by the first forty participants. When comfort care measures and hospice were discussed the responses were strong on "help us with our own feelings about death." Following the death education and communication programs many responses indicated, "We need to know more about pain and symptom control to help our dying patients." These nurses stated clearly that they want the philosophy and psychology of death education to be followed up by the practical "how to" information which they could utilize in their daily contacts with dying patients and their families.

A year ago I was given the opportunity at Valencia Community College to teach a 14-week death education course for student nurses. Entitled "Death, Dying, Loss and Grief", the course was set up originally in the traditional death education format because I felt the students might be overwhelmed if I also tried to incorporate communications skills, comfort care, etc.

The course was described as follows:

> This course is designed to gradually remove the social taboo of using such words as dead, dying, death, etc., so the student can fully explore the topics of death, loss, and grief with decreased anxiety.

> Focus of the discussion will be on the historical perspectives of death, the changing attitudes of today, developing a personal philosophy about death, the many types of loss, and the feelings which arise during the various stages of dying and the grief/loss reactions.

Objectives of the course were to:

1) Remove the taboo aspect of death language so the topic of death can be contemplated without great anxiety;

2) Examine the historical perspectives of death and dying and know how recent changes in attitudes affect treatment of the terminally ill;

3) Discuss the moral, ethical, and legal dilemmas created by the use of modern life support systems;

4) Become aware of how we feel about death--our own and that of others;

5) Learn how our feelings affect our relationships with terminally ill people and those who are recently bereaved;

6) Discover how children perceive and react to death;

7) Understand the stages in adjusting to the idea of dying and grief/loss reactions in order to help those who must cope with terminal illness or some type of loss;

8) Explore the concepts of past and current mourning rituals and learn why these practices are important to grief resolution;

9) Develop awareness of how unresolved grief reactions can produce both physical and mental health problems.

The class was limited to twenty-five people which I felt would be enough to provide diverse ideas for good discussion, but would not be too many for me to keep track of when it came to following up on students who might be having trouble handling their emotional response to these discussions. This turned out to be a reasonable working number. The class met for two hours once a week.

During the first class I asked everyone to fill in a short questionnaire telling me why they had signed up for the course, what they expected to gain from the experience, and what disturbed them most when they were faced with caring for a dying person. After explaining briefly the different types of loss people suffer, I asked them to indicate if they had had any significant loss in the past two years, and if so, the type of loss, month, and year. They could add any further explanation they felt appropriate.

At the bottom of the mimeographed sheet I had stated "This information will be kept confidential." I stressed this point several times in the hope that students would feel more comfortable disclosing this information. As those who have conducted death education courses know, there are usually a few hidden agendas among people who sign up for this course. It may be someone is searching for answers to a specific problem such as a recent loss or an impending one. It may be a concern for how to handle their own feelings about their own death or that of a beloved aging parent. Or they may have an unresolved grief situation of long standing. I find it helpful to try to get some inkling of these hidden agendas--or at least to be aware of who might possibly run into problems during the course. I still find there are always surprises along the way, however!

Also during the first class, we talked about keeping the details of our class discussions involving personal experiences confidential, just as we would information about our patients. Class members agreed to this. Several said later in the course they were glad we had stressed this confidentiality for otherwise they would not have felt they could talk openly about their death related feelings.

In the first weeks of class we covered the history of attitudes toward death and dying. This was followed by doing some of the death awareness exercises and discussion of feelings elicited by these exercises. As we got into the discussion of the emotional stages people may experience while going through a terminal illness, the student nurses expressed great concern over their inability to identify and respond appropriately to the needs of a person in a particular stage. They wanted to practice responding to patient situations so that when they were faced with the problem in the clinical setting of a patient denying their illness or someone depressed and crying all the time, they would have a little more confidence and skill to cope with the problem.

With the consent of the whole class, the original plan was changed and we spent the next five weeks role playing different situations.

Everyone had an opportunity to play both the "nurse" and the "patient" roles for each of the five stages. Each performance was followed by a critique of the "nurse's" responses and discussion of the feelings each performer had during the playing of the scene. In this way we covered most of the material originally planned for that part of the course, plus the students had a chance to try out their growing knowledge and skill in a safe, non-threatening environment. If students made mistakes, the rest of the group was right there with constructive suggestions and supportive reassurance, for everyone knew exactly how it felt to be in that role. Students rated this experience as the most helpful part of the course from a practical point of view.

Several students reported how this role playing had helped them in their clinical experience. One of the young women who worked part-time as an aide in an extended care facility (nursing home) said she was able to say a final goodbye to one of her favorite elderly patients before the lady died--something the student had often wanted to do with other favorite patients, but never had felt comfortable about actually doing. When asked how she felt about the experience, the student stated, "I feel like all the loose ends are tied up. I had known her for over a year and really loved her. I told her what a neat person I thought she was and how much I had learned from her. And she thanked me for taking such good care of her. We both cried, but it was okay." The lady had died the day after the conversation had taken place. The student was tearful when she shared this with the class, but she said she felt really good about her final conversation with her friend.

Another student reported how practicing active listening in class had helped in her personal life. She was very excited and could hardly wait to share with the class what had happened when her 80-year-old mother had made one of her frequent, complaint-filled phone calls the night before. The mother had a number of minor ailments common to elderly people. Every time she called her daughter she proclaimed how miserable she was, how hard it was to be alone, that she knew she was going to die any time now, and she hoped it would be soon so she would be out of her misery. In times past, the daughter, spurred by feelings of guilt and frustration, had replied brusquely, "Oh, don't be silly, Mother! You know the doctor has told you that you are in pretty good health for your age. You aren't going to die of these little aches and pains--you just have to learn to live with them." The conversations always ended in an argument with both mother and daughter upset, frustrated and angry.

On this particular occasion the daughter decided to apply her newly acquired listening skills. She encouraged her mother to ventilate her feelings, was supportive and sympathetic, acknowledged her feelings of loneliness and the frustration of coping with a body unable to work easily as it once did, and made a date to visit her the following Sunday. The conversation was calm and lasted about 20 minutes. Before saying goodbye, the mother thanked her daughter for listening to all her complaints. She added that she felt a lot better after talking awhile. The daughter was delighted that she was able to help her mother in this way. But, more than that, she felt some confidence in her ability to apply the communication skills she had practiced in class.

Another change in my original plans for the class came as a result of the clinical exposure the students had to terminally ill patients whom they felt helpless to make more comfortable physically. Knowing of my hospice nursing background, they asked many questions about comfort care, pain control, and the hospice concept of care. Again, with the consent of the whole class, we included these topics in the course.

At the end of the 14 weeks I realized we had covered all of the same material included in the courses I had previously developed for the continuing education for nurses classes. All of it proved to be as appropriate for student nurses as it was for those already in the work force. Using the revised lesson plan listed below, the course has been repeated with equally positive results.

Week 1 - Introduction and overview of course; testing and grading scale; instructor's expectations; student's expectations (verbal and written); personal information sheet completed.

Week 2 - History of and attitudes concerning death and dying; death systems of the past and present, rituals, and death denial.

Week 3 - Fear of death; nurses' fears; awareness of these fears and ways to overcome them. Assignment--write your will.

Week 4 - Life line exercise; discussion of feelings while writing will.

Week 5 - Stages in adjusting to the idea of dying; denial--role playing and communication skills.

Week 6 - Anger--as above.

Week 7 - Mid-term Exam, 30 minutes; bargaining--as above.

Week 8 - Depression--as above.

Week 9 - Acceptance--as above.

Week 10 - Hospice concepts of care for terminally ill people; comfort care, pain and symptom control.

Week 11 - Rituals, funerals, burial; visit from funeral director with question and answer period.

Week 12 - Children and death.

Week 13 - Ethical, moral, and legal issues.

Week 14 - Types of loss; grief reactions; resolution of grief; problems cause by unresolved grief.

Final Exam

The required reading for the course was On Death and Dying by Dr. Elisabeth Kubler-Ross. I chose this book despite the fact that it is required reading for part of the Nursing II class because the students have said in the past that they never got a chance in the nursing class to discuss all the ideas presented in the book. It proved to be an excellent springboard for discussion.

Along with role playing, I used a number of other methods to reinforce the learning process. Lecture time was kept to a minimum. Class participation was encouraged by many small group discussions. Structured learning experiences helped students examine their own feelings and attitudes and, hopefully, to develop and/or refine their philosophy about their own death.

Three books which I found particularly helpful in planning the structured learning experiences were:

Nursing the Dying Patient by Charlotte Epstein

Meeting Yourself Halfway by Sidney B. Simon

Thanatopics by Knott, Ribar, Duson, and King.

An on-going weekly class assignment to collect at least two examples of pictures, articles, cartoons, comics, stories, etc., from the printed media relating to any aspect of our discussion kept students aware of thinking about death and dying a part of the time between weekly sessions. Most of the material gathered in the first weeks of classes reflected the students' concern for sudden, violent death. In later weeks I encouraged them to look for death-related material other than crime, war, accidents, etc. They proved to be very resourceful. At the end of the course we had a fascinating collection ranging from the bizarre to hilarious to inspirational and covering every aspect of the subject.

Other materials used in this class were film strips and tapes produced by Trainex Corporation and Concept Media, the movie "A Time to Cry" rented from Mass Media Ministries, Baltimore, Maryland, and the film "Hospice--An Alternate Way to Care for the Dying", which is also available from Mass Media Ministries and some hospice groups.

In any death education class there will be those few students who will need some extra help to resolve the strong, disturbing emotions engendered by the discussions. I encourage my students to come talk to me if they find they are having difficulty with any aspect of the course. Several have taken advantage of this offer and, fortunately, most have been able to work through the problems. In one instance I realized very quickly the problem presented was outside my area of expertise. The student was willing to see one of the school counselors who then referred the student to a mental health agency which specializes in dealing with that particular problem.

When conducting the short courses I always announce at the beginning and the end of class that I will be available for individual questions or for those who might be feeling very uncomfortable as a result of the discussions. Also I try to be the last one to leave the classroom in case a particularly hesitant person has hung back until all others have left. I feel strongly that instructors must accept the responsibility to be available to troubled students. It is also our responsibility to know what resources are available to help students resolve the severe emotional problems which may surface as a result of the invitation to talk openly about death and dying.

Nurses are no different than any other group of human beings. Just because we have more contact with death and dying than most people does not mean that as a group we handle our reactions to death any better than members of non-health related professions. Unless nurses and nursing students are exposed to death education in a non-threatening environment there will be little progress made toward resolving those uncomfortable feelings engendered when faced with caring for a terminally ill patient.

Nurses and nursing students are different from other people who might enroll in a death education course in the need they have expressed to me to learn not only the basic death education information, but also knowledge and skills which will enable them to cope effectively with the diverse psychosocial and physical needs of the dying patient. As members of a caring profession, nurses want to know how to help this patient and the family members make the most of the time left available to them.

BIBLIOGRAPHY

Epstein, Charlotte. Nursing the Dying Patient: Learning Processes for Interaction. Reston, Va.: Reston Publishing, 1975.

Knott, J. Eugene, Ribar, Mary C., Duson, Betty M., & King, Marc R. Thanatopics: A Manual of Structured Learning Experiences for Death Education. Kingston, R.I.: SLE Publications, 1982.

Kubler-Ross, Elisabeth. On Death and Dying. New York: Macmillan, 1969.

Simon, Sidney B. Meeting Yourself Halfway. Allen, Tx.: Argus Communications, 1974.

EXERCISES ABOUT DEATH: FACT, FICTION, AND VALUES

Charles A. Corr
and
Donna M. Corr

The subject of this report is death-related exercises, exercises that explore participants' thoughts and feelings about death. Exercises of this sort are commonly introduced at the outset of Death and Dying courses, day-long workshops in the same subject area, or training courses for hospice staff and volunteers. We have employed many different exercises of this sort in our own teaching in a variety of contexts over a number of years. In view of the limits of this report, we will concentrate on a brief description of such exercises, an exploration of three issues which they raise, and some recommendations for their future.

The Exercises

The sort of exercise that we want to consider can take many different forms. For example, a well-known 1970 version in the journal, Psychology Today (1), asked readers to voluntarily fill out and send in a multi-item questionnaire on a variety of concerns about death. The journal received some 30,000 completed questionnaires, a response rate which far exceeded the same publication's earlier questionnaire about sexual attitudes. This death-related questionnaire and the interpretation of its results by Edwin Shneidman (2) was the subject of quite some interest in the early 1970's and, in a sense, is the modern parent of similar interrogation exercises.

About the same time, Robert Kastenbaum and Ruth Aisenberg in the first edition of their well-known book, The Psychology of Death (3), described various ways in which they had found that individuals would depict death, either as a person of one sort or another, or in some other form of drawing or visualization. In the same year, Shneidman published a journal article in which he asked whether young college students are capable of undertaking an exercise in writing their own obituaries (4). His use of such an assignment in a class at Harvard had generated a good deal of tension and widely divergent results. Some refused to undertake the task, others completed it but would not share the results with the instructor or the class, still others trudged through an unwelcome obligation, and a final group gave full reign to their creative imaginations.

Another option in this area is the so-called "do-it-yourself" death certificate in which individuals are asked to fill out their own death certificates using a reproduction of an actual form. Sabatini and Kastenbaum (5) have written about the use of such an instrument primarily as a research technique, while Michael Simpson (6) has reported on

Reprinted from Health Values: Achieving High Level Wellness, 1983, 7, 33-37, by permission of the publisher, Charles B. Slack Inc.

its use in a more pedagogical setting with health-care students in
Canada.   Other possibilities include role-playing of scenes such as
imparting information about a terminal diagnosis, a death-bed grouping,
or a funeral.

A full list of the sort of death-related exercises that we have in
mind is hardly possible. There is wide scope for creative imagination,
tempered only by some concern for the people who become involved in such
mental gymnastics. For our purposes here, enough has been said to
convey the essential character of the exercises that we have in mind.
Further examples or descriptions of many kinds of exercises like this,
together with some discussion of their use in teaching or group discussion settings, can be found in such sources as Robert Neale's The Art
of Dying (7), Charles Corr's article in the journal, Death Education,
outlining "A Model Syllabus for Death and Dying Courses" (8), and the
book, Thanatopics, by the past-president of The Forum for Death Education and Counseling, Gene Knott, and his colleagues (9). More sophisticated, but not altogether dissimilar, exercises are considered from
the standpoint of research methodology by Richard Schulz (10) and in the
section on "Research and Assessment of Death Attitudes" in Death Education: An Annotated Resource Guide (11, pp. 133-145).

Although there are many possible types of opening exercises related
to death, our focus in this report is on those of the "paper-and-pencil"
sort. From among the many of these which we have used, we select two
for discussion and comment here. They are the do-it-yourself death
certificate and an exercise in which participants are asked, in one way
or another, to describe the moment of their death. The former exer-
cise--the do-it-yourself death certificate--tends to provide more organized and clearly defined data because of its structure, but it also is
somewhat more confrontational in character than other possibilities. It
is mildly surprising how many people in our society--even professional
caregivers--have never seen a death certificate, surely one of the basic
documents of modern societies. Because this document is so foreign to
daily life and because it requires precise and detailed data, many
people who are presented with this exercise find themselves unable to
enter into it or unwilling to complete it fully. Obviously, their
feelings must be respected. Exercises of any sort which concern death
can be expected to generate some tension in nearly all participants--in
a sense, that is their very point--but they should not be too coercive
and care must be taken not to go beyond manageable bounds.

An exercise in which people are asked to imagine the moment of
their death and to describe it on a blank or unstructured piece of paper
is a bit less formidable. The main reason for this is that such an
assignment is more open-ended in permitting participants to determine
the manner and length of their response. One might strengthen that
element of control in another way by phrasing the task somewhat differently. For example, one could stipulate a situation in which the
individual had the ability to control all of the relevant variables
entering into his or her projected death, and then ask: How would you
choose to die in such circumstances? Or--more interestingly for some
people--How would you wish not to die?

McLaughlin and Kastenbaum (12) have described a two-phase exercise
in which participants are asked to describe the moment of their death on
one sheet of paper, set that aside and erase it from their minds, and
then repeat the exercise with a different description of the day of
their death on a second sheet of paper. Obviously, this somewhat more
sophisticated approach is intended to penetrate early facades in the
hope of reaching deeper and perhaps truer concerns, and the testers
appear to have had good results with its use. Our own experience with
this procedure has not yielded very significant variations (though that
outcome may itself be worthy of attention), but we have usually had
neither time nor a suitable context to employ and exploit complex
exercise techniques. Researchers or those with training in testing
methodologies who have suitable populations and contexts may heighten
the quality of exercise results, but we believe our outcomes are more
likely to accord with typical experiences of educators and trainers.
For that reason, we only address here relatively unsophisticated uses of
death-related exercises.

When we have employed do-it-yourself death certificates and exercises requiring projected descriptions of the moment of one's death, we
have generally observed a clear and dominant pattern of response.
Typically (especially in younger persons), death is placed quite far off
from the present time (e.g., towards the end of the 21st century), and
accompanied by the hope that it will occur quickly or even instanta-
neously, without pain, and in one's sleep. In other words, we have
noted about our respondents a fairly common desire to postpone or
distance death as far as possible, and a wish once it is about to occur
to have it take place without much time for or trauma in dying. A
sizeable group of Mid-Western respondents expresses the desire to die
when one has made one's peace with God, i.e., to die when "ready" in a
religious or theological sense. Only a small minority mention family or
those who will survive, but such individuals often give very detailed
and thoughtful responses.

The Issues

We select for presentation here three issues which arise from these
sorts of death-related exercises. They are: 1) compliance; 2) content;
and 3) interpretation. With regard to compliance, many individuals, as
indicated above, simply will not or cannot undertake exercises of this
sort. Particularly in "captive" audiences or those which are not
self-selected, being asked to confront the thought of one's own death in
a serious way can be an unusual demand in our contemporary society and
may provoke significant anxiety or resistance. We have found college
students to be more compliant in this respect than Shneidman did some
ten years ago at Harvard, but older, more mature people or those who are
less accustomed to being submissive to classroom instructors display a
higher rate of noncompliance and recalcitrance. In general, over the
many years in which we have used death-related opening exercises, we
have noticed a gradually increasing willingness to entertain such
devices and to cooperate with their requirements. That does not,
however, undercut our warning about problems with compliance, nor our
recommendation that great care and, where possible, prior preparation be
employed in using these sorts of exercises with any audience.

Some people may start an exercise of this sort, but find themselves unable to finish it. For the researcher, such folk do not produce "useable" results, although exploration of abortifacient factors within the encounter may be most useful for educators, trainers, and participants themselves. Apparently, as these last individuals enter into the assignment, it becomes for them increasingly confusing, threatening, or unrealistic. In particular, for the do-it-yourself death certificate, participants may simply not know how to respond to some questions or what information is appropriate. In any of these exercises, some people seek compulsively for the "right" answer. Other uses humor as a distancing or protecting device. Where permitted, many talk among themselves so as to reach out to comrades and disspell isolation. Another caution in relation to compliance is that even when the project is completed, the achievement may be based on an idiosyncratic perspective. For example, one woman said that filling out her own death certificate was easy for her for the very good reason that in real life she would never expect or be able to write such a document for herself. When asked how the task could have been made more realistic and perhaps more fruitful, she promptly replied: if I had to fill one out for my husband!

Very recently, we have been coming into contact with individuals who have been participants in a number of death-related exercises as a result of having attended more than one course or workshop on this subject. Less virginal populations of this sort are increasingly more likely in view of the spread of educational activities in the field of death and dying. When confronted with repeated death-related exercises, such individuals report contrasting reactions: some are bored by what they view as sterile redundancy; others find in the exercises new perspectives and opportunities for increased growth. Obviously, these reactions depend to some extent on the kinds of exercises and the ways in which they are employed. Educators and trainers must be alert to changes in the people with whom they are dealing, and to the implications of differences between or alterations within subject populations for compliance with death-related exercises.

Closely related to issues of compliance are those concerning the character of the data resulting from death-related exercises. In our experience, the data or content of all such death-related exercises are often unrealistic. This seems to result mainly from uncontrollable shifts between what participants expect will take place at the time of their death to what they wish will occur. The former emphasis appears most evidently in considerations such as age at the time of death, location and cause of death, and method of disposition of the body. Certainly for younger populations all of the present demographic statistics may change by the time they reach their acutal death, but likely projections concerning average life expectancy, home vs. institutional locus of death, and burial vs. cremation—to cite just three examples—do not usually accord with results of the exercises that we have seen. And in some important ways, these initial or ostensive results may not even be desirable when viewed from a larger or more thoughtful perspective. We think it unlikely that ambivalence between desires and expectations can ever fully be removed from exercises of this sort. As noted above, some suggest that such ambiguities simply be accepted and directly explored by way of incorporation into the process through such techniques as multi-phase exercises. That strategy may be desirable. Our own approach as educators and trainers is to make the ostensive content of the exercises, along with the process itself, a subject for discussion with participants. In this way, we involve participants in both a mutual and an individual process of extended exploration and reflection. The goal is not to rule out "unrealistic" data or to coerce participants in any particular direction, but simply to create additional opportunities for increased self-understanding and growth.

Consider, for example, the marked preference shown with regard to manner of death for fast, painless, even unexpected death, i.e., for death (if is must occur) without dying. This emphasis is so prominent that even among professional caregivers we have found inordinate efforts to avoid cancer as a cause of death, to the point of preferring (pain-less?) heart attacks in great disproportion to their actual occurrence. After reporting to a group such data with regard to cause of death as given in their exercises, we might ask them why they appear to be so energized in this particular way. Another illustration of skewing in the content of death-related exercises is seen in what appears to be their dominant focus of concern. Mode of death in such exercises usually reflects an overriding preoccupation with self-satisfaction vs. the interests of family members or other probable survivors. Why is this? Perhaps such exercises only ask or seem to ask about one's self? But are any of us as independent of other persons as such responses might suggest? Unanticipated, instantaneous deaths in our society are often precisely those which are hardest on survivors, and one only has to mention that after an exercise to initiate a richer reflection which may yield different results from those initially offered.

A third important--and, again, a related--issue is that of inter pretation. To begin with, there are numerous limitations to paper and pencil exercises for issues related to death. Even the color of the paper used can affect the resulting data, as we discovered when we once inadvertently distributed blank sheets of pink paper which reminded some participants of blood! Shifts between expectations and preferences, and concerns related to "unrealistic" data have already been mentioned above, but take on new prominence when it comes time to interpret any results which might follow upon them. Moreover, even on an anonymous page it is problematic what individuals are willing to share merely because some stranger has asked them to do so. More importantly, it is not clear how much anyone is able to share about thoughts and feelings which touch us as deeply as those related to death and our own mortali-ty. On this point, we need to remind ourselves of what Richard Schulz (10, p. 25) has called "problems of the unitary concept assumption." That is, concerns abut death are manifold and diverse. For example, Michael Simpson (13) has distinguished in "death anxiety" fears of four general types (fears of dying, fears of death, fears of the results or consequences of death, and fears of the death or dying of others) and many subordinate modes. We have difficulty in identifying and sharing our own thoughts and feelings related to death precisely because they are made up of multiple, overlapping, and changing elements.

Our point for this discussion is that data which emerge from opening death-related exercises are far from absolute. Such data are subject to all of the usual potential for interpretational error, as well as to special cautions relating to their specific focus of concern. They may provide an entry-point or a place to begin for educators and trainers, as well as for the individuals who participate in our exercises. But is is quite uncritical to assume that such data necessarily afford an accurate or a complete portrait of intertwined cognitive, affective, behavioral, and valuational dimensions of an individual's involvement with death. Thus, the interpretation of data generated by short-term death-related exercises is in itself a very hazardous business indeed.

The Moral

The principal conclusion that we draw from our experience with opening death-related exercises is twofold: First, that the data or results which they yield may not be very reliable in themselves; but second, that the process of conducting and carrying out such exercises is nevertheless still quite valuable as such. For the first point, in 1973 a Swedish physician named Gunnar Biorck wondered in print "if there is a tendency in the modern Western society to wish for a sudden, unexpected death--why then make great efforts to try to deprive people of this privilege?" (14, p. 605). This line of thought seems to suggest that we should survey preferences regarding death in fairly random populations not under imminent threat of dying using exercises roughly of the sort under discussion here, and then as a society or as caregivers take action to implement such putative desires. Apart from issues of the moral, social, or professional responsibilities of independent agents, this recommendation is naive and dangerous. It falsely assumes a high degree of reliability in data which are often quite superficial, and it posits in the participants a firm grasp of their own basic attitudes and considered preferences regarding death. We want to be far more cautious in any dependence on or use of the results of death-related exercises.

A variant of this first point appears in the tendency of some researchers and teachers to use opening exercises as benchmarks for measuring changes or (worse yet) "progress" in alteration of death-related attitudes. Again, reliability is suspect, but more importantly it is very questionable whether Death and Dying courses, hospice training programs, and other similar short-term workshops and courses which deal with the deep and complex topic of death should conceive themselves as designed to alter attitudes related to death. Marcia Lattanzi has questioned this very point in a discussion of hospice training programs and their goals (15). Are we really in the business of altering death-related attitudes? Can we expect to achieve such a large-scale outcome in short-term learning situations? Do we even know enough about death-related thoughts and feelings or their formation to know how one might go about altering them? We think there is a lot to be said, at least right now, for a negative response to all three of these questions.

Our enduring conviction with regard to death-related exercises is that in the end it is the process which really counts, not the ostensive results. What such exercises actually do is help to initiate a process of personal exploration or to extend a self-reflective inquiry. That process is particularly valuable in a culture where it has too often been avoided or discouraged. The process may assist individuals toward long-term change in their own death-related attitudes. But it is the individual who will be the primary agent in altering his or her own attitudes, for better or worse and however that may be defined. Life experiences can influence that process, and death-related exercises can be a very tiny component of such experiences. But educators and trainers normally play a far less direct or significant role in that process that they might like to think. If individuals who participate in death-related exercises only come to learn in this way more about their own thoughts and feelings regarding death and to realize that such thoughts and feelings will play a role in all of the relationships that they engage in with other people or situations, then the exercises will have done their job and will have achieved the limited ends that are within their scope of influence.

REFERENCES

1. Shneidman, E.S. Death questionnaire. Psychology Today, 1970, 4, 3, 67-72.

2. Shneidman, E.S. You and death. Psychology Today, 1971, 5, 1, 43-45, and 74-80.

3. Kastenbaum, R., & Aisenberg, R. The psychology of death. New York: Springer, 1972.

4. Shneidman, E.S. Can a young person write his obituary? Life-Threatening Behavior, 1972, 2, 262-267.

5. Sabatini, P., & Kastenbaum, R. The do-it-yourself death certificate as a research technique. Life-Threatening Behavior, 1973, 3, 20-32.

6. Simpson, M. The do-it-yourself death certificate in evoking and estimating student attitudes toward death. Journal of Medical Education, 1975, 50, 5, 475-477.

7. Neale, R. The art of dying. New York: Harper & Row, 1973.

8. Corr, C.A. A model syllabus for death and dying courses. Death Education, 1978, 1, 433-457.

9. Knott, J.E., Ribar, M.C., Duson, B.M., & King, M.R. Thanatopics: A manual for structured learning experiences for death education. Kingston, R.I.: SLE Publications, 1982.

10. Schulz, R. The psychology of death, dying, and bereavement. Reading, MA.: Addison-Wesley, 1978.

11. Wass, H., Corr, C.A., Pacholski, R.A., & Sanders, C.M. Death education: An annotated resource guide. New York: Hemisphere, 1980.

12. McLaughlin, N., & Kastenbaum, R. Engrossment in personal past, future and death. Paper presented at the annual meeting of the American Psychological Association, New York City, September, 1966. Reported in #3 (above), pp. 34-35.

13. Simpson, M. Social and psychological aspects of dying. In H. Wass (ed.) Dying: Facing the facts. New York: McGraw-Hill/Hemisphere, 1979, pp. 108-136.

14. Biorck, G. How do you want to die? Answers to a questionnaire and their implications for medicine. Archives of Internal Medicine, 1973, 132, 605-606.

15. Lattanzi, M. Learning and caring: Education and training concerns. In C.A. Corr & D.M. Corr (eds.) Hospice care:

principles and practice. New York: Springer, 1983, pp. 223-236.

THOMAS ATTIG is Professor and Chairperson of the Department of Philosophy at Bowling Green State University in Ohio. Attig is currently Acting Treasurer of the Forum. His book, Ethics and the Environment (co-edited with Donald Scherer) was published by Prentice-Hall in 1983.

CHARLES A. CORR is Professor in the School of Humanities of Southern Illinois University at Edwardsville. He co-edited (with Hannelore Wass) Helping Children Cope with Death: Guidelines and Resources published by Hemisphere in 1982.

DONNA M. CORR is Instructor in the Nursing Faculty of St. Louis Community College at Forest Park. She is co-editor (with Charles A. Corr) of Hospice Care: Principles and Practice published by Springer in 1983.

EVA K. BROWN CRANDALL is Assistant Professor, School of Nursing, Washburn University, Topeka, Kansas.

KENNETH J. DOKA is Associate Professor in the Gerontology Program at the Graduate School of the College of New Rochelle, New York, and a Lutheran Clergyman. His articles have appeared in several professional journals.

JEANNE M. HARPER teaches at Marinette Catholic Central High School in Wisconsin. She is a Board Member of Forum and has published in two previous proceedings volumes.

PATRICIA A. HYLAND has extensive experience both as a psychiatric nurse and as a psychiatric social worker. She lives and works in Topeka, Kansas.

GERALD G. JAMPOLSKY is founder of the Center for Attitudinal Healing in Tiburon, California.

NATHAN R. KOLLAR is Professor of Religious Studies and Gerontology at St. John Fisher College in Rochester, New York. His book, Songs of Suffering, was published in 1982 by Winston Press.

LOUIS E. LaGRAND is Professor of Health Science at the State University College of Arts and Sciences, Potsdam, New York.

BONNIE LINDSTROM is Bereavement Coordinator, St. Mary's Hospice (formerly Hillhaven Hospice), Tucson, Arizona.

MARGARET SHANDOR MILES is Professor, School of Nursing, University of Kansas, Kansas City, Kansas, and is widely known for her work on parental bereavement. Her booklet, The Grief of Parents When a Child Dies (1980) is now distributed by The Compassionate Friends.

MARY C. RIBAR teaches English at Eastern Intermediate School in Montgomery County, Marland. She is co-author (with J. Eugene Knott,

Betty M. Duson, and Marc R. King) of Thanatopics: A Manual of Structured Learning Experiences for Death Education (SLE Publications, Kingston, Rhode Island, 1982).

SHIRLEY SCOTT is a nurse who has worked with cancer patients both in the hospital setting and in a hospice home-care program. Currently, she is an instructor in the Valencia Community College Nursing and Continuing Education Programs in Florida.

EDWIN S. SHNEIDMAN is Professor of Thanatology, Department of Psychiatry, University of California at Los Angeles.

JUDITH M. STILLION is Professor of Psychology at Western Carolina University, Cullowhee, North Carolina. Her book, Death and the Sexes, will be published by Hemisphere in early 1984.

HANNELOR WASS is Professor of Educational Psychology at the University of Florida, Gainesville, and editor of the journal, Death Education. Her next book, Childhood and Death (co-edited with Charles A. Corr) will be published by Hemisphere early in 1984.